# Secondary Teacher Training

# Secondary Teacher Training

Ajoy Chatterjee

CRESCENT
PUBLISHING CORPORATION

*[The responsibility for the facts stated, conclusions reached and plagiarism, if any, in this book is entirely that of the Author. And the Publisher bears no responsibility for them, whatsoever.]*

**Secondary Teacher Training**



Edition : 2018

ISBN 81-8342-056-7

*Published by:*

**CRESCENT PUBLISHING CORPORATION**
4806/24, Mathur Lane,
Ansari Road, Darya Ganj,
New Delhi - 110002
Ph.: 011-23244131
Mob.: 9711991838, 9999021668
e-mail : crescentbook@gmail.com
Website : www.crescentpublishingcorp.weebly.com

*Printed at :*
**Balaji Digital**
Delhi

# Preface

A secondary school teacher teaches one or more national curriculum subjects to classes of pupils aged 11-16 or 11-18. The subjects are determined by the national curriculum but how they are taught is down to the professional judgement of the teacher, whose priority it is to ensure pupils learn. Teachers develop schemes of work and plan lessons in line with national objectives. They encourage, monitor and record the progress of individual pupils and devise and adapt resources to suit their own students.

The usual route into secondary teacher education is the completion of a degree qualification followed by a one-year Diploma of Teaching (Secondary). There are also some four-year programmes for secondary teaching which incorporate the degree qualification and teacher education within the same programme. In recent years secondary teacher education has been offered by a range of universities and private teacher education establishments. This has increased the number of places throughout the country where teacher education can be accessed. There are now many more options for part-time, remote, campus-based and specialist programmes.

This book comprehensively describes the problems and methods of secondary teacher training. It is divided into ten chapters. It is hoped that this book will prove useful to the teaching departments and institutions, teachers of educational administrations as well.

*Ajoy Chatterjee*

# Contents

# 1

# Modern Instruction Strategies

The use of active learning techniques have a positive impact upon students' learning. For example, several studies have shown that students prefer strategies that promote active learning rather than traditional lectures. Other research evaluating students' achievement has demonstrated that many strategies promoting active learning are comparable to lectures in promoting the mastery of content but superior to lectures in promoting the development of students' skills in thinking and writing.

Some cognitive research has shown that a significant number of individuals have learning styles best served by pedagogical techniques other than lecturing. Development and implementation of these techniques requires that teachers become knowledgeable about active learning strategies and alternative approaches to instruction.

When instructional strategies are tied to the needs and interests of students, learning is enhanced. Instructional strategies should be directly tied to the curriculum, desired student outcomes, and classroom assessments.

## Development of Mnemonic Strategies

Mnemonic strategies do not represent a "philosophy" of

education. We do not use, or recommend the use of, mnemonic strategies because they are compatible with someone's particular philosophy or because they are a part of someone's theory about what education should be. We recommend mnemonic strategies for only one reason: Over and over again, they have been proven to be extremely effective in helping people remember things. It is also true that mnemonic strategies are not an overall teaching method or curricular approach. The focus of mnemonic strategies is so specific that they are intended to be used to enhance the recall of the components of any lesson for which memory is needed. We have found, for example, that mnemonic strategies can be used to enhance science learning when the curriculum involves a textbook/lecture format or when the curriculum involves a hands-on, inquiry learning format.

Even though these approaches to science learning are very different, mnemonic strategies can still be incorporated for the elements that require recall. It is also important to consider that mnemonic strategies are memory strategies, and not comprehension strategies. Students who are trained mnemonically also perform better on comprehension tests of that content, but that is generally because they remember more information that can be applied on comprehension tests. Nevertheless, when comprehension enhancement is called for, it is important to consider using specific comprehension strategies, such as content elaboration, prior knowledge activation, manipulation, coaching and questioning, or prediction and verification.

Nevertheless, mnemonic strategies do not inhibit comprehension, as suggested by some, and, more importantly, there are many instances in school of students who have achieved adequate comprehension of a concept, but who have forgotten the facts associated with it.

Mnemonic strategies do not represent an educational panacea. There are many things that students must do to succeed in school, and remembering content information is only one part of the entire picture. However, when there is academic content to be remembered, mnemonic strategies may be an important instructional component.

## Procedures for Memory Improving

Mnemonic strategies are not the only way of improving memory in students who exhibit difficulty remembering things. It is important that you consider all possible methods for improving memory and not assume that mnemonic strategies are your only option. In other publications, we have described more general methods for improving memory. These include the following:

### *Increase Attention*

Students will not remember something that they did not pay attention to in the first place. Be sure your students' memory problems are not really attention problems. Use strategies for enhancing attention, such as intensifying instruction, teaching enthusiastically, using more visual aids and activities, and reinforcing attending.

### *Promote External Memory*

Many things that need to be remembered can be written down, a practice known as "external memory." Practices such as keeping an assignment notebook and maintaining a student calendar can be helpful in remembering to do things. Unfortunately, external memory is usually of little use (ethically, anyway) on tests.

### Enhance Meaningfulness

Find ways to relate the content being discussed to the student's prior knowledge. Draw parallels to the students' own lives. Bring in concrete, meaningful examples for students to explore so the content becomes more a part of their experience.

### Use Pictures

Pictures can provide a memory advantage. Use pictures on the chalkboard or on the overhead projector. Bring in photographs or other illustrations. Show concrete images on videotape, when appropriate. If pictures are simply unavailable, ask students to create images, or " pictures in their heads."

### Minimize Interference

Avoid digressions and emphasize only the critical features of a new topic. Make sure all examples relate directly to the content being covered.

### Promote Active Manipulation

Students remember content better when they experience it for themselves. For example, rather than lecturing the class on the effect of weak acid (such as vinegar) on calcite, allow students to place calcite in a glass of vinegar and see for themselves.

### Promote Active Reasoning

Students remember better if they actively think through new information, rather than simply repeating it. For example, rather than simply telling students that penguins carry their eggs on the tops of their feet, ask students why it makes sense that penguins would carry their eggs on the tops of their feet.

*Increase the Amount of Practice*. Students remember information better if they have practice using it more frequently. Use lots of review in your teaching; do not simply finish one topic and then never mention it again. Remind the class, and have students practice previous information frequently. All these strategies can be used to improve memory, and all should be considered. Unfortunately, none of these strategies specifically targets recall of information contained in new or unfamiliar words, and this is the aspect of memory where students most often fail.

## Techniques for Mnemonic

### *Keyword Method*

The keyword method has already been described for helping students remember states and capitals. However, the keyword method is extremely versatile and has a variety of helpful applications. One possibility is in teaching new vocabulary words. For example, to help students remember that barrister is another word for lawyer, first create a keyword for the unfamiliar word, barrister. Remember, a keyword is a word that sounds like the new word and is easily pictured.

A good keyword for barrister then, is bear. Then, you create a picture of the keyword and the definition doing something together. It is important that these two things actually interact and are not simply presented in the same picture. Therefore, a picture of a bear and a lawyer in one picture is not a good mnemonic, because the elements are not interacting. A better picture would be a bear who is acting as a lawyer in a courtroom, for example, pleading his client's innocence.

The keyword method can also be used for more specialized vocabulary such as ranidae the scientific term for common frogs. A good keyword for ranidae could be rain and you could show a picture of frogs sitting in the rain. Practice the strategy as in the barrister example. When you question individual students, ask them to give the answer and then describe how they remembered. You should get an answer something like: Ranidae is the word for common frogs. Because the keyword is rain and it was raining on the frogs.

If you practice the strategy carefully and frequently, students should remember this information very well. At early stages of learning, you might find some students give the answer rain when you ask what ranidae means. Mnemonics can also be used in acquiring foreign language vocabulary. Keywords have also been used to improve recall of map locations. For example, students with learning disabilities were much more successful in locating Revolutionary War battle locations on a map when they were mnemonically encoded than when representational pictures were used. When asked for the location of Fort Ticonderoga, students proved much more able to identify where on the map the tiger had been than they were to identify the location of a more traditional illustration.

### Pegword Method

Pegwords can be used when numbered or ordered information needs to be remembered. Pegwords are rhyming words for numbers and include the following:

- One is bun six is sticks
- two is shoe seven is heaven
- three is tree eight is gate
- four is door nine is vine
- five is hive ten is hen

Pegwords are substituted for the number to be remembered and associated with the other information. For instance, to remember that insects have six legs whereas spiders have eight legs, create a picture of insects on sticks and another picture of a spider on a gate. To remember Newton's first law of motion, create a picture of a bun (pegword for one) resting. To remember that a garden rake is an example of a third-class lever, create a picture of a rake leaning against a tree. Pegwords can also be combined with keywords. To teach that crocoite is a mineral that is number 2 on the Mohs hardness scale, create a picture of crocodiles (key-word for crocoite) wearing shoes (pegword for 2).

To remember that the mineral wolframite is hardness number 4, black in colour, and used in making filaments for lightbulbs, create a picture of a black wolf (keyword for wolframite), looking in a door (pegword for 4), and turning on a lightbulb. Research has shown that elaborate strategies such as this are very effective, and that color, appropriately encoded, can also be easily remembered. Pegwords can also be extended beyond the number 19, by using, for example, twenty is twinty (twins), thirty is thirsty, forty is party, and fifty is "gifty," or gift-wrapped. For example, to remember the math fact, 7 x 8 = 56, create a picture and practice the pegword phrase, "Heaven's (7) gate (8) holds gifty sticks". To remember that Taft was the 27th president, create a picture of a taffy (keyword for Taft), being pulled between twin heavens (pegword for 27).

## LETTER STRATEGIES

Letter strategies, which involve using letter prompts to remember lists of things, are the most familiar to students. Most former students remember using the acronym HOMES to remember the names of the Great Lakes and FACE to remember the notes represented in the spaces of the treble clef, from bottom to top. Except for the FACE strategy, however, most acronyms assume that a name of something will be remembered when the first letter is retrieved. However, this may not always be true. For example, if a student is unfamiliar with Lake Ontario, remembering simply that the first letter is O is insufficient to prompt recall. The names of the individual lakes must be practiced until they have become familiar.

For example, if you wished to remember the names of the planets in their order from the sun, the letters would be M-V-E-M-J-S-U-N-P, from which a word cannot be made. In these cases, an acrostic can be created, in which the first letters are reconstructed to represent the words in a sentence. In this case, the sentence could be "My very educated mother just sent us nine pizzas". Again, the names of the planets must be sufficiently familiar so that students can retrieve a planet name, given only the first letter. Also, students should be sufficiently familiar with the solar system to know that the first M stands for Mercury, and not Mars.

### *Training of Students with Mnemonic Strategy*

Several research studies have described the effects of training students with memory problems how to use mnemonic strategies independently. The earlier studies successfully trained students with disabilities to use the mnemonic procedures and then to generalize the procedures for learning new vocabulary words. More recent studies trained students with disabilities to use the strategies across different content areas, including science and social studies. All of these studies demonstrated some positive benefits for training students to use mnemonic strategies independently. More importantly, however, studies shared seven common elements during the training sessions with students with disabilities.

*Step 1.* Inform students about the purpose of the instruction and the rationale for the strategy training. Tell students that strategy training will be beneficial for them and that their efforts at using the strategies will result in better performance. Provide examples of how the strategy can be beneficial across a variety of learning situations and content areas. For example, in teaching students how to implement the strategy to learn science vocabulary, show them how the method can also be helpful in learning social studies content and for learning English and foreign language vocabulary.

*Step* 2. Provide instruction in the strategy and in positive attributions toward strategy usage. Demonstrate, model, and lead students using many examples to ensure their complete understanding of the mnemonic process during the strategy component training. Provide instances and noninstances of correct usage and have them identify and correct any incorrect examples.

Make charts listing the steps involved in generating strategies. King-Sears et al. taught students the IT FITS strategy:

- Identify the term.
- Tell the definition of the term.
- Find a keyword.

– Imagine the definition doing something with the keyword.

– Think about the definition doing something with the keyword.

Provide ample modeling and practice with students, attributing their successes to strategy use. Say, for example, "When I try hard and use the strategy, I will remember more information." Reinforce students for trying hard to use the strategy and attribute success and failure to strategy usage.

*Step 3.* Provide models during which examples and thinking processes are said aloud. Demonstrate how you proceed with your thinking while generating a strategy for specific examples. Include statements attributing your success to the hard effort and use of the strategy.

*Step 4.* Allow students opportunities to practice orally and provide corrective feedback. Practice several examples with the class as a whole. Encourage brainstorming during the development of the keyword and interactive picture phase. Allow students to work in small groups and practice generating strategies and brainstorming. Then, have students work with partners to develop strategies before working independently.

*Step 5.* Arrange guided practice with relevant feedback on both strategy usage and attribution feedback. Give students additional items to practice using the mnemonic and attribution strategies. Provide corrective feedback and allow opportunities for students to share their thinking with one another about how they developed their strategies.

*Step 6.* Provide generalization instruction, practice, and feedback. Use different types of materials to demonstrate how the strategy can be applied across content areas and various types of factual information. Have students practice generating strategies for vocabulary words in English, for names of famous people and their accomplishments in history, for minerals and their associated attributes in science, and other associated factual information they may need to learn in school.

*Step 7.* Include positive reinforcement and positive attribution training for completing the tasks and for remembering the information correctly. Provide review and practice with information that was learned using strategies. Students will still need to practice retrieving information learned with strategies. When implemented as a package of training, students with disabilities may be more likely to learn to use and generate these strategies independently.

Research has indicated that students who have been taught strategies for creating their own mnemonics outperform comparison students in free-study conditions. Unfortunately, however, when students generate their own strategies, instruction may proceed at a much slower rate and students' performances may be lower than when teachers supply the strategies. During a given unit of instruction, teachers should consider whether learning a strategy or learning the content is the priority. Moreover, initial development of many of these strategies can be difficult for anyone.

Try developing several strategies yourself before teaching your students with disabilities. If you experience difficulties, imagine that the task will be much more difficult for your students. Each year, develop a few strategies to accompany the content areas that you teach most frequently. Over time you will have a great number of effective strategies that you can teach your students. This does not mean that you should not teach your students to develop strategies independently. You can still encourage active strategy development on the part of your students, but if students have difficulties generating strategies, you can supply the ones developed by you or your co-teachers. Perhaps you will find that a combination of teacher-created and student-generated mnemonic strategies is the best way to enhance recall and still promote independent strategy use.

## MAKING OF MEMORABLE INSTRUCTION

Three explosions are simultaneously vibrating through the schools and classrooms. First is an explosion of content information to be taught. Second is an increased emphasis on student learning outcomes. Third is the growing number of students with learning and attention difficulties who struggle with grasping new concepts and retaining information over time. Consider the following instructional strategies, which are designed to maintain student interest, maximize student engagement, and optimize the memory of content information over time.

1 *Grab their attention.* Employ a variety of introductory activities or "attention grabbers" to stimulate student interest in the learning task. Stress ways that the content to be taught is meaningful or applicable to students' lives and outside interests.

2 *Make it relevant.* State a clear purpose and objective for each lesson. Tell students exactly what you expect them to be able to accomplish following each teaching segment. Stress goal attainment so that students recognize and take pride in their own progress.

3 *Do it together.* Stress the active engagement of students in their learning process. Encourage them to correct

their own mistakes and to learn from them. Use any mistakes that you make as "teachable moments." Encourage cooperation rather than competition so students seek ways to be coaches and study buddies for one another.

4 *Try teams.* Utilize the social needs of your students for added motivation. Many students will work harder for the success of a peer group than they would when working alone. Use learning teams whose members are rotated regularly. Students can practice the interpersonal skills required to work effectively with different individuals as they achieve essential learning outcomes.

5 *Take aim.* Teach goal setting and encourage students to set their own realistic goals. You can help by providing a realistic range. These short-term goals are easily met, yet are stepping stones to larger achievements.

6 *Keep it visual.* Teach students to monitor and graph their progress toward the goals that they select. Simple graphs provide excellent visual displays and documentation of student progress. As an added benefit, these graphs are good learning activities in themselves.

7 *Create a schemata.* Take time to explore students' prior knowledge before teaching a new concept or skill. Become an expert in creating bridges from students' past experience to new learning. Emphasize ways that new content relates to students' prior knowledge as well as to content that you have presented in class.

8 *Think big.* Stress the relationship and use graphics to visually display the link between superordinate concepts or global ideas. Less skilled learners, in

particular, may fail to see the relationship between topics unless these are stated explicitly.

9 *Draw it out.* Employ a variety of graphic organizers. Charts, diagrams, maps, and semantic webs are examples of visual displays that are useful for facilitating learning and memory. Generic templates can be easily modified for use across content areas.

10 *Show them how.* Provide numerous examples, models, and illustrations of the new concept or skill. Be sure to include more complex problems as well as some straightforward examples. Ask students to create additional problems for each other and for the class.

11 *Stimulate the cognitive.* Use "think-alouds" as you demonstrate the steps to a new process or procedure. Tell students exactly what you are thinking and why as you employ each step. The key is to verbalize explicitly those self-regulating cues that you would normally perform automatically. Consider the needs of skill "novices" and try to prevent areas of difficulty with specific instruction.

12 *Teach a trick.* Stress the use of mnemonic techniques for improved memory. In some cases, first-letter acrostics may be devised. In other cases, keyword mnemonics may be used for associative information. To remember that Taft was president when federal mail service was established, select a keyword that is familiar to students. Second, think of an interaction between the word and the answer. Use the steps to recall Taft and the establishment of mail service.

13 *Talk out loud.* Coach students to elaborate as they reason through topics that follow logical sequences or action-reaction formats. Encourage students to problem-solve by asking probing questions-"Why does

it make sense that. . . " or, "The fishing industry is big business in ... ? "

14 *Build on what they know.* Use scaffolded learning by providing very detailed instruction and materials during early learning. Offer less scaffolding as learners become more skillful with the content. Once you have modeled a procedure on numerous occasions, you can prompt students to become more independent in their use of this technique.

15 *Keep the action going.* Employ a variety of methods for actively involving students in practicing their new skills. Small dry-erase boards and individual chalk or game boards provide excellent opportunities for guided practice and allow additional feedback to students.

16 *Make a note.* Teach students to take lecture notes using a series of guided steps. For the earliest lessons in note taking, provide a structured outline that requires students to fill in the blanks. In subsequent lessons, gradually decrease the amount of information that you provide and require increased levels of student input.

17 *Think ahead.* Encourage students to make predictions, to summarize, and to monitor their comprehension as they read independently. After direct instruction of these reading strategies, students can be prompted to use and practice comprehension skills across content areas.

18 *Practice, practice, practice.* Provide lots of opportunities for students to practice a new skill. These can take the form of coaching activities or other relevant practice methods.

19 *Clinch new learning.* Use specific closure activities to complete a learning segment or lesson.

20 *Refresh their memories.* Provide systematic review for the content you teach. Even the most motivating instruction will not be remembered unless it is reviewed in a systematic way. Research supports the use of distributed rather than massed practice. Devise a schedule of weekly review sessions and be sure to include games or other activity-based formats.

## Scholastic Assessment Test (SAT)

The Scholastic Assessment Test (SAT) scores of students with learning disabilities are significantly lower because of the characteristics inherent within the disability itself. A learning disability is a "disorder in one or more of the basic psychological processes involved in understanding or in using language, spoken or written, that may manifest itself in an inability to listen, think, speak, read, write, spell, or to do mathematical calculations". Other traits may include uneven and unpredictable test performance, perceptual impairments, and low tolerance for frustration.

Because the SAT taps into every aspect of this definition and traits-with the exception of spelling-the student with a learning disability is at a high risk for a low score unless he or she is thoroughly prepared for all demands of the test, from filling out the answer sheet and coping effectively with test anxiety, to managing time and choosing which questions not to answer.

### *Metacognitive Strategies*

META-TEST is a two-part SAT test-taking strategy, based

on the principle of metacognition, or thinking about thinking. Students with disabilities can be inefficient in evaluating the correctness of their own responses (self-appraisals) and can evidence persistent helplessness in developing self-help strategies (self-management). Metacognition addresses these two difficulties because it emphasizes the student as an "active learner," one who asks questions, makes decisions, and exercises control over the learning process.

Studies have shown that although all students benefit from strategy instruction, metacognition emphasizes personal appraisal and management, lending itself to the individual strengths and weaknesses of students with learning disabilities. META-TEST differs from traditional large-group SAT instruction because, first, it is a personal approach that correlates a student's learning strengths and weaknesses with the myriad individual tasks required during an administration of the SAT. Second, the student is accountable for developing and presenting his or her own personal test-taking strategy. The end result is tailor-made for maximum effectiveness.

The school district, parent, and student can truly feel that the student is "ready" to take the test. Fortunately, the student with a learning disability has a wealth of personal information to aid him or her in preparing for the SAT. This information emanates from the student's psychological report and the individualized education programme (IEP):

- The psychological report identifies the exact nature of the learning disability in terms of academic strengths and weaknesses, as well as discrepancies in test scores such as vocabulary, reading, and math computation and problem solving-essential components of the SAT. In addition, it identifies personal learning styles and makes recommendations for compensatory techniques for the child to be successful. It also examines and explains other factors that may interfere with test-taking ability, such as difficulty following directions, distractibility, or processing weaknesses.

– The student's IEP contains important information regarding current functioning levels, academic successes, complete and incomplete annual goals, and daily physical or management needs, as well as a transition plan that may include college preparation.

### META-TEST SAT

The junior year of high school should be devoted to serious test preparation, beginning with a meeting among the student, parent, guidance counsellor, and special educator. Here the ground rules for the SAT Contract are presented. This meeting should summarize the intent and process of this step-by-step approach, as well as emphasize the partnership necessary for success. Because each contract is individualized according to the nature of the student's learning disability, the special educator should act as the coordinator because he or she knows the student's ability and disability best. Completing the contract will enable each student to develop his or her own personal test-taking strategy.

The goal of the META-TEST Contract is to establish an ongoing dialogue between coordinator and student. Paris and Winograd explained that "dialoguing" is an important aspect of "scaffolded instruction, " the goal of which is to provide the learner with just enough support to achieve a goal that would initially be impossible without support, as well as "cognitive coaching," the goal of which is self-regulated learning.

Students with learning disabilities need to manage their own learning by planning, evaluating, and regulating their performance on academic tasks. The SAT Contract consists of a series of steps, each ending with the coordinator's signature of approval, date, and any necessary recommendation. The first step is knowledge of the test format, a sort of overview of the test, a sense of the gestalt. The student must be able to explain and/or list the following: the number of Verbal and Math sections, the number of questions in and content of each section, and the amount of time allotted for each section. This explanation helps the student plan the pace of the SAT and is an integral part of self-regulated learning. This increasing familiarity with format will reduce test anxiety.

### *Test Directions*

Knowledge of test directions is important because students may only work on one section of the test during a specific period of time. Test directions are greatly influenced by whether or not the student takes a standard timed administration or nonstandard administration with testing accommodations. The presence of an IEP or 504 Plan does not automatically mean that a student is eligible for testing accommodations.

In general, test accommodations must parallel those used on classroom and schoolwide tests, and may include extended time, largetype test book and answer sheet, Braille device, cassette test, a reader to dictate test questions, or a writer to record responses.

#### *Test-Taking Tips*

Some of the top test-taking tips for students with disabilitiesgiven below:

- Know the test directions because for every 5 minutes you spend reading directions, you will have fewer minutes to answer questions.
- Do the easy questions first because they are equal in point value to difficult ones.
- Know how the test is scored because you get one point for each correct answer and lose a fraction of a point for each wrong answer. You can get an average score by just answering about half the questions correctly.
- Omit questions that you have no idea how to answer.
- Review and complete a practice answer sheet.
- Be careful filling in the grids.
- Take and evaluate a Practice SAT (PSAT).

These tips affirm the credo of professional SAT preparers that knowledge of good test-taking strategies can reduce anxiety and improve test scores.

*Taking a Practice Test*

The most important step in completing the SAT Contract is taking a diagnostic practice exam. The exam should simulate actual testing conditions, timed or untimed. The coordinator should note offtask ,behaviours and distractibility and discuss these with the student when the exam is reviewed to determine how to effectively use break time. The student should learn how to score the exam and determine a Verbal and Math score. The student and the coordinator should carefully review each section of the exam to determine the student's strengths and weaknesses.

*Personal SAT Strategy Development*

During the evaluation of the practice exam, the student and

the coordinator discuss and complete the student's Personal SAT Strategy. The student should be able to explain or list his or her personal strengths and weaknesses; this evaluation will help the student examine and practice these questions at a later date during an SAT Review class where individual questions and problems are discussed. Many students use the PSAT to accomplish this goal, in addition to a practice SAT. Outlining a Personal SAT Strategy is perhaps the most important step in this process because it brings together all information in a meaningful way. It specifies the following:

- Exactly what aspect of the student's learning disability from the psychological report should be the focus of the strategy.
- What accommodations are required according to the recommendations on the student's IEP or 504 Plan.
- What specific strategy should be used on the Verbal and Math sections to maximize strengths and minimize weaknesses.

Because the student has been an active part of this process, he or she should feel "enabled and empowered" to be successful. Finally, the student should explain his or her Personal SAT Strategy either orally or in writing.

### *Students' Practice*

After the student has completed a Personal SAT Strategy, he or she is ready to concentrate on the types of individual questions through a SAT review course, learning centre, resource room, or local curriculum. It is never too early to provide students with the skills necessary for the SAT. One virtue of metacognition is that the constructive, personal, strategic thinking it embraces is amenable to classroom instruction on all levels for all students. The curriculum of English, social studies, and science classes should include analogy and sentence-completion type questions in their weekly exams. Reading comprehension passages similar in content and format to the SAT can be provided in all content area classes. Math classes, in addition to teaching students how to problem solve, must also present questions in the varied format of the SAT.

## Differentiation of Instruction

In most elementary classrooms, some students struggle with learning, others perform well beyond grade-level expectations, and the rest fit somewhere in between. Within each of these categories of students, individuals also learn in a variety of ways and have different interests. To meet the needs of a diverse student population, many teachers differentiate instruction.

At its most basic level, differentiation consists of the efforts of teachers to respond to variance among learners in the classroom. Whenever a teacher reaches out to an individual or small group to vary his or her teaching in order to create the best learning experience possible, that teacher is differentiating instruction. Teachers can differentiate at least four classroom elements based on student readiness, interest, or learning profile:

(1) *content*—what the student needs to learn or how the student will get access to the information;

(2) *process*—activities in which the student engages in order to make sense of or master the content;

(3) *products*—culminating projects that ask the student to rehearse, apply, and extend what he or she has learned in a unit; and

(4) *learning environment*—the way the classroom works and feels.

### Content

Examples of differentiating content at the elementary level include the following:

(1) using reading materials at varying readability levels;

(2) putting text materials on tape;

(3) using spelling or vocabulary lists at readiness levels of students;

(4) presenting ideas through both auditory and visual means;

(5) using reading buddies; and

(6) meeting with small groups to re-teach an idea or skill for struggling learners, or to extend the thinking or skills of advanced learners.

### Process

Examples of differentiating process or activities at the elementary level include the following:

(1) using tiered activities through which all learners work with the same important understandings and skills, but proceed with different levels of support, challenge, or complexity;

(2) providing interest centres that encourage students to explore subsets of the class topic of particular interest to them;

(3) developing personal agendas (task lists written by the teacher and containing both in-common work for the whole class and work that addresses individual needs

of learners) to be completed either during specified agenda time or as students complete other work early;

(4) offering manipulatives or other hands-on supports for students who need them; and

(5) varying the length of time a student may take to complete a task in order to provide additional support for a struggling learner or to encourage an advanced learner to pursue a topic in greater depth.

### *Products*

Examples of differentiating products at the elementary level include the following:

(1) giving students options of how to express required learning (e.g., create a puppet show, write a letter, or develop a mural with labels);

(2) using rubrics that match and extend students' varied skills levels;

(3) allowing students to work alone or in small groups on their products; and

(4) encouraging students to create their own product assignments as long as the assignments contain required elements.

### *Learning Environment*

Examples of differentiating learning environment at the elementary level include:

(1) making sure there are places in the room to work quietly and without distraction, as well as places that invite student collaboration;

(2) providing materials that reflect a variety of cultures and home settings;

(3) setting out clear guidelines for independent work that matches individual needs;

(4) developing routines that allow students to get help when teachers are busy with other students and cannot help them immediately; and

(5) helping students understand that some learners need to move around to learn, while others do better sitting quietly.

Students in the elementary grades vary greatly, and if teachers want to maximize their students' individual potential, they will have to attend to the differences. There is ample evidence that students are more successful in school and find it more satisfying if they are taught in ways that are responsive to their readiness levels, interests and learning profiles. Another reason for differentiating instruction relates to teacher professionalism. Expert teachers are attentive to students' varied learning needs; to differentiate instruction, then, is to become a more competent, creative, and professional educator.

The most important factor in differentiation that helps students achieve more and feel more engaged in school is being sure that what teachers differentiate is high-quality curriculum and instruction. For example, teachers can make sure that:

- curriculum is clearly focused on the information and understandings that are most valued by an expert in a particular discipline;
- lessons, activities, and products are designed to ensure that students grapple with, use, and come to understand those essentials;

- materials and tasks are interesting to students and seem relevant to them;
- learning is active; and
- there is joy and satisfaction in learning for each student.

One challenge for teachers leading a differentiated classroom is the need to reflect constantly on the quality of what is being differentiated. Developing three avenues to an ill-defined outcome is of little use. Offering four ways to express trivia is a waste of planning time and is unlikely to produce impressive results for learners. There is no recipe for differentiation. Rather, it is a way of thinking about teaching and learning that values the individual and can be translated into classroom practice in many ways. Still, the following broad principles and characteristics are useful in establishing a defensible differentiated classroom:

- *Assessment is ongoing and tightly linked to instruction.* Teachers are hunters and gatherers of information about their students and how those students are learning at a given point. Whatever the teachers can glean about student readiness, interest, and learning helps the teachers plan next steps in instruction.
- *Teachers work hard to ensure "respectful activities" for all students.* Each student's work should be equally interesting, equally appealing, and equally focused on essential understandings and skills. There should not be a group of students that frequently does "dull drill" and another that generally does "fluff." Rather, everyone is continually working with tasks that students and teachers perceive to be worthwhile and valuable.

– *Flexible grouping is a hallmark of the class.* Teachers plan extended periods of instruction so that all students work with a variety of peers over a period of days. Sometimes students work with like-readiness peers, sometimes with mixed-readiness groups, sometimes with students who have similar interests, sometimes with students who have different interests, sometimes with peers who learn as they do, sometimes randomly, and often with the class as a whole.

In addition, teachers can assign students to work groups, and sometimes students will select their own work groups. Flexible grouping allows students to see themselves in a variety of contexts and aids the teacher in "auditioning" students in different settings and with different kinds of work

#### *Differentiation Guidelines*

Teachers are as different as their learners. Some teachers naturally and robustly differentiated instruction early in their careers. For other teachers, establishing a truly flexible and responsive classroom seems daunting. It is helpful for a teacher who wants to become more effective at differentiation to remember to balance his or her own needs with those of the students. Once again, there are no recipes. Nonetheless, the following guidelines are helpful to many teachers as they begin to differentiate, begin to differentiate more proactively, or seek to refine a classroom that can already be called "differentiated":

1. Frequently reflect on the match between your classroom and the philosophy of teaching and learning you want to practice. Look for matches and mismatches, and use both to guide you.

2. Create a mental image of what you want your classroom to look like, and use it to help plan and assess changes.

3. Prepare students and parents for a differentiated classroom so that they are your partners in making it a good fit for everyone. Be sure to talk often with students about the classroom—why it is the way it is, how it is working, and what everyone can do to help.

4. Begin to change at a pace that pushes you a little bit beyond your comfort zone—neither totally duplicating past practice nor trying to change everything overnight. You might begin with just one subject, just one time of the day, or just one curricular element (content, process, product, or learning environment).

5. Think carefully about management routines—for example, giving directions, making sure students know how to move about the room, and making sure students know where to put work when they finish it.

6. Teach the routines to students carefully, monitor the effectiveness of the routines, discuss results with students, and fine tune together.

7. Take time off from change to regain your energy and to assess how things are going.

8. Build a support system of other educators. Let administrators know how they can support you. Ask specialists (e.g., in gifted education, special education, second language instruction) to co-teach with you from time to time so you have a second pair of hands and eyes. Form study groups on differentiation with like-minded peers. Plan and share differentiated materials with colleagues.

9. Enjoy your own growth. One of the great joys of teaching is recognizing that the teacher always has more to learn than the students and that learning is no less empowering for adults than for students.

## Strategies for Vocabulary Instruction

When you think of vocabulary, there is a good chance that you think of long lists of words from social studies or science textbooks, spelling word lists, or even the humongous lists of terms to study for college entrance exams. Zillions of flash cards also may come to mind. No doubt you share the common childhood experience of having to "go look up the words in a dictionary, write the definition, and then write a sentence using the term" – but how much of that vocabulary do you remember now? Do you remember how you could rote copy the definition of a term as part of a homework assignment, but have no real idea what the definition meant and still get an 'A' on the assignment?

Perhaps the least effective way to study vocabulary is the "look and remember" technique. Here, students typically stare at the term and definition, apparently trying to activate photographic memory they wish they had. Another common study technique is 'rote verbal rehearsal' – saying the word over and over again, usually in the exact language and format from which the definition originally came. Many of the traditional techniques teachers and students use to learn vocabulary does not work because most students, not just those with learning problems, rarely remember the meanings of new terms beyond the test.

This raises a very disconcerting question: If students don't remember the definitions of new terms after the test, why bother requiring them to memorize these definitions in the first place since it seems to be a waste of time? New terms must be defined using language and examples which are already familiar to students, and that the more ideas from background knowledge with which the student can associate the new term, the more likely it will become well 'networked' and permanent part of memory. There are a variety of tactics and strategies that can be mediated by the teacher to help students understand and remember new terms as well as the significance of important names, events, places, or processes. All of these tactics involve facilitating elaboration in various ways.

### *Elaboration Techniques*

There are several elaboration techniques that appear to be particularly powerful facilitators of comprehension and memory of new terms. These are briefly described below.

1. Teach new terms in context of a meaningful subject-matter lesson, and facilitate student discussion that centres on use of the new term. At some point, students should use the new term themselves in a sentence within the context of discussing broader topics. The traditional practice of having students look up definitions and then write sentences using the new terms likely stems from the idea that students must think of the term and create a context for which it might be appropriately used. While composing written sentences clearly is an important elaboration technique for the learner, essential to also include in the learning process is learning about the term within an overall context so that relational understanding can develop.

   Although providing opportunities for students to elaborate about new terms requires a significant portion of class time, it is clearly a worthwhile instructional practice. The problem is, students are often expected to memorize the definitions of far more terms than there is time in class to elaborate upon. To provide meaningful opportunities for elaboration, we need to teach considerably fewer terms, and invest considerable more time in developing deep knowledge structures of those that are really essential for students to know. This means that students are typically expected to memorize far too many terms each week.

Another implication of this first elaboration technique is that the common practice (often associated with language arts classes) of having students attempt to learn long lists of un-associated words without the benefit of learning them within some meaningful context is largely a waste of the teacher's and student's time.

2. Facilitate paraphrasing of new term's definitions so that students can identify the core idea associated with the overall meaning of the term, as well as distinguish the new term's critical features. If you were to dissect the semantic structure of a new term, you would find that its definition actually has two main components:

   (i) The core idea of the new term is like its 'gist' or main idea; and

   (ii) critical features of the definition are specific bits of information in the definition that clarify the broader, more general core idea. This is analogous to paraphrasing main ideas of paragraphs when reading in which the reader says what the overall paragraph was about (main idea) and indicates important details in the paragraph. With new terms, the goal is to paraphrase the core idea of the term and identify specific critical-to-remember details that clarify the core idea.

3. Make background knowledge connections to the new term. While teaching the new term in context of a subject-matter lesson is a critical instructional technique, an equally important elaboration technique is for students to relate the term to something in which the students are already familiar. There is a wide array of methods by which students can formulate knowledge connections. For example, they can identify how the term is related to previous subject-matter they have learned, they can identify something from their personal life experiences the term reminds them of, they can create metaphors or similes for the term, or they can say how the term relates to understanding or solving some form of real-life problem. An essential part of this elaboration process is having the students explain the connection.

4. Identify examples/applications as well as non-examples/non-applications related to the new term's meaning. Comprehension is greatly enhanced if the learner can accurately identify examples of the term or ways the new term can be appropriately applied within the context of discussing another context. For example, the term 'peaceful resistance' might be used when describing Martin Luther King's approach to solving racial discrimination problems. You will likely find that students' comprehension of new terms becomes considerably more focused and refined if they can also identify examples of what the term is not about or inappropriate applications of the term's use. Having the student discuss of what the term is not an example, or other concept with which someone should not confuse it, can facilitate this.

5. Create multiple formats for which students can elaborate on the meaning of new terms. Many teachers will utilize all of the above elaboration processes within the context of a class discussion, and yet some students still do not seem to 'get it.' This is because the manner in which elaboration was facilitated was all 'lipear', or verbal or listening, forms of instruction. Writing elaborations, even for those where scripting is a laborious process, creates an opportunity for greater reflection on the term's meaning. Other forms of elaboration involve use acting out via role-play the meanings of some terms or creating mnemonic pictures or stories that capture the essence of a new term's meaning.

### *Clarifying Routine*

The Clarifying Routine focuses on ways each of the above forms of elaboration can be facilitated. The teachers uses an instructional tool, called a Clarifying Table, to facilitate these kinds of thinking behaviours. The teacher can use the Cue-Do-Review sequence when applying the Routine.

#### *'DO' Instruction*

The 'Do' component of this routine can be very effectively applied in four basic ways adapted from Anita Archer's characterization of scaffolded instruction: 'I do it' (model), 'We do it' (provide guided practice), and 'You do it' (independent practice).

*'I do it' instruction*: The purpose of the first phase of 'Do' instruction is to provide students with a precise model of a well-constructed Clarifying Table depicting information related to an essential new term students need to learn. The first time students are introduced to Clarifying Tables, the

usually provide them with one that he/she have completely constructed ahead of time, and just walk them through it in much the same manner as he/she might explain the information depicted on a web or other pre-constructed graphic organizer. After explaining the information depicted on the Clarifying Table, he/she usually ask students what they like about the table and how well it helps them understand the meaning of a new term. The teacher typically do this twice before moving to the next phase, 'We do it.'

*'We do it' instruction*: During 'We do it' instruction, the teacher co-constructing Clarifying Tables with students. Although he/she may have constructed one for a new term prior to class as part of his/her planning process, so my instruction will go smoothly, he/she will not show students a completed version. Rather, he/she first teach the meaning of the new term in the context of a subject-matter lesson, and then provide students with blank copies of a Clarifying Table. Together, they (students and the teacher), decide what ideas should be noted on the form. Thus, the whole class decides on what to note as the "Core Idea" for the new term, what to list as "Clarifiers," "Knowledge Connections," and so forth.

'We do it' forms of instruction continue through the year, thus the teacher never really stop co-constructing Clarifying Tables with students. As students become more confident and competent at constructing these tables, however, his/her role tends to shift from being the person who frequently cues students what to do and helps them actually phrase ideas to note on the form to a role that is much more like a "guide-on-the-side."

*'Yall do it' instruction*: Once it becomes evident to the teacher that most students understand purpose of the

Clarifying Table and can construct them with little assistance from him/her, he/she begin incorporating cooperative learning activities where students work in pairs or small teams to construct Clarifying Tables without teacher assistance. While it varies depending of the nature of the class, the teacher usually begin incorporating 'Yall do it' activities after we, as a class, have constructed between five and ten Clarifying Tables.

Naturally, the more familiar students are with the meaning of the new term, the easier it is for them to construct a Clarifying Table. Thus it is very important that the teacher do a great job teaching the new term's meaning in the context of his/her subject-matter lesson before he/she ask students to work together to construct a Clarifying Table. 'Yall do it' activities allows students to have some support, but the nature of the support comes from peers rather than the teacher.

*'You do it' instruction*: The Clarifying Table is a versatile tool that teachers can use to teach the meanings for new terms, and students can use as a strategy for independently studying new terms. 'You do it' activities are designed to enable students to perform this task without assistance from others. An example would be requiring students to construct Clarifying Tables for five terms in lieu of requiring them to complete traditional study guides or answer the end-of-chapter textbook questions.

Assignments that require students to independently construct Clarifying Tables only occur, however, after a sufficient amount of scaffolded instruction has previously occurred. A very common mistake is to jump from providing an initial model (I do it) to requiring students to independently do it themselves (You do it) without the intermediate guided practice mediated by the teacher and by peers.

## Effective Instructional Resources

A key feature of effective teaching is the selection of instructional materials that meet the needs of students and fit the constraints of the teaching and learning environment. There are many pressures for educators to match the audiovisual stimuli of television, computers, and electronic games with which students are experienced. The speed of personal computers and the ease of authoring systems permit instructors to design and customize computer-based audiovisual presentations and to develop computer-based assignments for their students. The tremendous increases in rates of information transfer, access to the Internet, and posting of materials on the World Wide Web give instructors and students an almost limitless supply of resource material. In addition, the ease of electronic communications between an instructor and students, and among students, provides new opportunities for sharing questions, answers, and discussions during a course.

At the same time, there remains a major role for student use of textbooks and for instructional use of demonstrations, films, videos, slides, and overhead transparencies. Carefully scripted presentations and activities run the risk of emphasizing teacher delivery rather than student learning. Carefully planned and prepared instructional resources sometimes tempt instructors to race ahead and to cover more. The rapid-fire presentations combined with audiovisual overload can tempt students to remain intellectually passive.

One way to avoid this is to intersperse activities which assess student understanding and encourage reflection and critical thinking. Another possibility is to reduce the pace of the class session, by pausing periodically to invite questions. Instructional resources usually fall into one of two categories: student-centered and teacher-centered. In the student-centered model, instructional resources can be used for tutorials, problem solving, discovery, and review. Information technology can also be used for communication and for information retrieval.

### Using Textbooks

The mode of teaching so common today—the lecture-text-exam approach—is an artifact of centuries of European education. The professor's main role before the wide availability of the printing press was to lecture on information obtained from a rare copy of an often ancient book. Books are a highly portable form of information and can be accessed when, where, and at whatever rate and level of detail the reader desires. Research indicates that, for many people, visual processing (i.e., reading) is faster than auditory processing (i.e., listening to lectures), making textbooks a very effective resource. Reading can be done slowly, accompanied by extensive note taking, or it can be done rapidly, by skimming and skipping. There are advantages to both styles, and you may find it useful to discuss their merits with your students.

One important aspect of any science class is helping the student to make sense of the mass of information and ideas in a field. This can be done by showing students how to arrange information in a meaningful hierarchy of related major and minor concepts. Well-chosen textbooks help students understand how information and ideas can be organized. Textbooks have several major limitations. Although a well-written book can engage and hold student interest, it is not inherently interactive.

However, if students are encouraged to ask questions while they read, seek answers within the text, and identify other sources to explore ideas not contained in the text, they will become active readers and gain the maximum benefit from their textbook. In order to meet the needs of a broad audience, texts are often so thick that they overwhelm students seeking key information. Texts are often forced to rely on historical or dated examples, and they rarely give a sense of the discovery aspects and disorganization of information facing modern researchers.

### *Style and Content of Textbook*

Science textbooks have evolved considerably from the descriptive and historical approaches common before World War II. Today's texts are far more sophisticated, less historical, and contain more facts than in the past, with complex language and terminology. Illustrations and mathematical expressions are more common. Emphasis has shifted toward principles and theory. Modern texts attempt to deal with issues of process as well as matters of fact or content. They are replete with essays, sidebars, diagrams, illustrations, worked examples, and problems and questions at many different levels. One result of these changes is that the average book length has increased two to four times in the past several decades.

In response to the need for quality science textbooks for all students, not just science majors, some authors are returning to descriptive and historical approaches. Generally, books for science literacy courses describe important ideas and discoveries, present a limited number of fundamental concepts, and emphasize the links among different facts and principles. Others take an interdisciplinary approach, by covering a range of science disciplines in a coherent, connected manner.

### *Textbooks Learning*

Research on the effectiveness of textbooks has focused on two general areas: text structure and layout. The study of text structure has focused on how the reader builds cognitive representations from text. Recent work categorizes the structure of science text as either a proof-first or a principle-first organization. The proof-first organization develops a proof or argument that builds to a conclusion, usually in the form of a fundamental concept, principle, or law. In principle-first organization, a concept or principle is stated explicitly, then the evidence needed to support it is presented. The prevalence of the proof-first structure in contemporary textbooks may be due to the fact that most college science textbooks are written by scientists with little formal training in education. They present science the way it is practiced by experts.

However, studies by Dee-Lucas and Larkin indicate that the principle-first structure is more effective for long-term retention and understanding by novice readers. Layout and illustrations are important predictors of a text's effectiveness. One of the most effective types of illustration, especially for students with low verbal aptitude, is a simple multicolor line drawing. Although more visually appealing, and more prevalent in the current textbook market, realistic drawings or photographs are less effective at enhancing student learning. The organization of information on a page also affects student learning.

### *Selecting Appropriate Textbook*

Before selecting a text, it is important to know what books are currently on the market. Colleagues who teach the same or a similar course are good sources of ideas and information. Your campus bookstore's textbook manager can provide the name and phone number for textbook sales representatives from many different companies. Science education publications carry advertisements from major publishers, and some feature a book review section or annual book buyer's guide. Professional society meetings also provide a chance to talk to publishers and see their new textbooks. Many companies will supply review copies to potential textbook adopters, in return for information about the course in which it might be used.

There are a number of factors to consider when selecting a textbook. To be of greatest value to students, the objectives of a textbook must be consistent with those of the course. Authors often try to meet particular objectives in their books, and these may differ among the choices. Skim the preface to see whether you share the author's approach to the subject. Consider how the table of contents aligns with your course syllabus and teaching philosophy:

- Is coverage of topics broad or specific?
- Are key principles stated precisely and clearly?
- Are the explanations and interpretations consistent with your teaching style?

In addition to content, evaluate the text structure and layout as discussed in the previous section. Textbooks vary greatly in their level of difficulty with respect to readability, depth of theoretical treatment of information, and complexity of end-of-chapter problems. Colleagues who have adopted the book can provide insight about these issues. They are also helpful for determining whether a textbook contains errors, which have been shown to have a large, negative effect on student learning.

### *Use of Textbook*

Following are the suggestions for hows to use a textbook:

- Study assigned readings before each class. Be prepared for questions, references to those readings, and other activities building on that material.
- Take notes in outline form as you read the text, indicate key points with a highlighter, note connections between sections, make lists of questions that come to mind or uncertainties, and pause frequently to summarize the key points of each section or chapter.
- Compare your lists of questions and your lists of key points with those of others in the class.
- Bring questions to class or recitation sections and ask the instructor to answer them.
- Review the text after the class to gain additional perspective.
- Look in supplemental texts to see how other authors present similar topics, especially if the points seem vague or unclear in the primary text. Remember that often the presentation that introduces new information, concepts, and vocabulary will seem foreign. Another presentation with a slightly different twist may help you see something differently or may confirm that you have identified key points.
- Review the text before exams and quizzes or periodically throughout the term.
- Study and review worked examples before attacking the homework problems. Read over questions, exercises, and problems that are not assigned and think about how to answer them. Group questions or problems by the topics they address or the methods

required to solve them. Summarize by writing your own problems. Consult worked examples in other texts.

## Use of ICTs

### *Internet*

The Internet is an international high-speed electronic communications network (linking many local, regional, and national networks) which allows individuals at institutions or at home to access each other's computers for rapid communication or information retrieval. For some, the value of the Internet is that it allows users at remote locations to sign-on to computers where they have accounts, often using connection software called telnet. For others, rapid electronic communication and document sharing replaces phone conversations and meetings and facilitates collaboration.

Another major use of the Internet has been to provide free public access to documents in electronic form. Many individuals and organizations "post" documents on their own computers so that others can obtain electronic copies. File transfers can be made by FTP (file transfer protocol) software, and for many who have posted documents to their Web pages, file transfers can be initiated by as little as the click of a button on the title of the document.

### *World Wide Web*

The World Wide Web (WWW) is a system of linking information (text, sound, graphics, and video) in a way that allows for easy movement between related documents and sites. To use the Web you need a computer with special software that is called a browser, such as Lynx, Mosaic,

Cello, or Netscape, or equivalent services available through commercial Internet providers. Highly detailed text, graphics, and videos are available on a wide array of topics. The Internet and the ease of information viewing and retrieval that are possible through the Web mean that students are no longer limited to information provided by textbooks and printed materials in libraries.

Students may "search" on the World Wide Web for preprints and reprints of articles, for discussion bulletin boards on specialized topics, for conference abstracts and proceedings, or for topical compilations of materials for research or teaching. Most Web navigational software systems include search engines that allow the user to locate information or sites by topic area. With more than a thousand new Web sites added every day, browsing for information on the Web needs to be done even more carefully than a literature search for library references. Bear in mind that while the Web holds enormous potential in providing access to information, much of the information available has not been reviewed for quality or reliability.

A number of electronic resources are available to those seeking information about education. Many professional societies have created Web pages with information about their educational initiatives and with links to other resources.

### *Electronic Communication*

Electronic mail ("e-mail") enables students and faculty to communicate with each other and with people all over the world. Many groups have adopted or created systems under which messages sent to a single address are delivered to mail accounts of all members of the group. This kind of electronic bulletin board is called a "listserv." A variation of a listserv bulletin board is a moderated listserv for which all messages are viewed by a moderator (and perhaps condensed, grouped, arranged, and/or edited) before being broadcast. Another form of group electronic communication is through a bulletin board on which messages are posted, called a newsgroup.

Interested readers must sign on to a particular electronic address to find and read messages or posted documents. Bulletin boards of this type permit readers to leave their reactions to and comments or the postings of others. Many instructors use electronic communication to facilitate interactions among students, and between students and themselves. Some faculty members create course-related Web pages with a mechanism for students to enter their comments or messages when they are connected to the Web page. Sample uses of e-mail or Web pages for communication include:

- Students send questions electronically to the instructor, which gives them an opportunity to express a doubt or misconception that they might have been afraid to voice in class. The instructor can transmit the question and the answer simultaneously to all students, without identifying the individual who asked the question.
- Students send or post questions about course material and are encouraged to answer each other's questions. Faculty members can monitor these exchanges to gauge student understanding and progress.
- Faculty hold "electronic office hours" in addition to traditional ones, so that students can ask a question and receive an answer almost immediately. This approach is becoming more common at institutions with a large commuter population, where students

cannot always attend the faculty member's office hours.

- Faculty require drafts of student papers to be submitted electronically; not only does this make it easier for some faculty to review the draft, it forces the student to become familiar with technology used in the workplace.
- Faculty members distribute or post homework assignments, homework solutions, exam solutions, and other supplemental information electronically.
- Faculty create electronic "suggestion boxes" where students can post their comments about the course; consult the administrator of your campus e-mail system for ways to make the postings anonymous.

# 2

# Classroom Observation

Students with a learning disability and/or an attention deficit disorder usually find the normal hum of classroom activity extremely distracting. Even such tiny, unavoidable sounds as turning pages, shuffling feet, and whispered conversations catch their attention and draw their minds away from schoolwork. When left to their own devices, LD/ ADD students tend to use background music to filter out normal environmental noises. They usually like to play the radio, the stereo, or the television when they want to concentrate.

They also find it helpful to work in an area where they can spread out, move around, and be comfortable. Body postures other than sitting up straight at a desk help them to "get into" what they are doing. Standing at the blackboard, kneeling on the floor, leaning back in a chair, perching on a stool, pacing around the room, or hunching over a workbench, a countertop, or a drawing table-any position that increases wholebody involvement is likely to help these youngsters pay attention to their work.

When studying at home, they tend to prefer spreading out on the dining-room table or sprawling on the couch, bed, or floor. By taking note of the modifications these youngsters provide for themselves, teachers can make adjustments in the classroom environment to help LD/ADD students overcome many of their difficulties with paying attention in class. In a carefully controlled atmosphere, the LD/ADD pupil has his best chance for successful learning. Distractibility and a short attention span are major causes of the LD/ADD youngster's classroom disasters.

## Location for Classroom

Regardless of age, LD/ADD students usually have an attention span significantly shorter than that of their classmates. Because their periods of concentration are so brief, they frequently look up from their work and check on what's going on around them. If there is something interesting nearby, it captures their attention so that they never return to their work. For teacher, the trick is to seat pupils with a learning disability and/or an attention deficit disorder where there is little of interest to hold their attention when it's not focused on schoolwork.

A seat in the front of the room is often best. This limits what's in the student's line of vision. Instead of seeing a whole room of interesting bulletin boards plus thirty or more active bodies, he sees only the front third of the room, the blackboard, and a few classmates. If the pupil is situated on the extreme left or right side of the front row, distractions can be cut to a minimum. However, front row corner seats present special problems which must be taken into consideration. Areas of heavy traffic and frequent activity should be avoided. If the teacher's desk, the wastebasket, and the pencil sharpener are on one side, the LD/ADD child should be on the other. When the choice is near the door or near the window, the door is usually the less distracting of the two.

College students with a learning disability and/or an attention deficit disorder almost always have less trouble paying attention in class when seated in the front of the room and off to one side. When seated in the middle or back of a lecture hall filled with two hundred or three hundred students, they notice every person-what they're wearing, what they're doing, where else they've been seen around campus-and little attention is left for watching the instructor, listening to the presentation, and taking notes. In young children, this tendency to notice everything going on around them can be a tremendous handicap. For those few who simply cannot screen out the sights and sounds around them, any class of more than six or eight students makes concentration totally impossible! No amount of medication, classroom modification, or one-to-one instruction can enable them to tune out the other students and keep their minds on their schoolwork. Such children can make a shambles out of a tranquil classroom.

With the "inclusion" law and small LD classes rarely available, parents of these highly distractible youngsters are faced with the choice between homeschooling and private school. Leaving severely distractible children in regular classrooms is far too destructive to the child-not to mention to his teacher and his classmates-to be given serious consideration. Some LD/ADD students should not be placed in the first row of a classroom. For those who are hyperactive and those with serious behaviour problems, sitting in front of an entire class makes them actors with an audience. When the distractions that disturb them are limited, they become the distraction that disturbs everyone else. This must not be allowed.

Overactive children-whether medicated or not-wiggle, bounce, tap, twist, hang out of their chairs, wander around the room, and race to the teacher's desk. Most of the time, they are playing with something in their hands. Almost always, they are in motion. Medication often helps them contain their excess energy, but as a general rule it is pointless to try to control their level of activity. The most effective approach is to limit their territory.

Hyperactive students usually are least disruptive if seated at one end of the back row. This location also provides them the extra amount of physical freedom they need. Rather than wasting her time and energy trying to keep such youngsters in their seats, the teacher can concentrate on confining their activity within reasonable but specific bounds. It is effective to give such young sters an adjusted set of rules: "You may move freely about this area of the room, provided you do your work, don't do anything dangerous, and don't disturb others." The exact limits of their territory should be made absolutely clear. With young children, it may be necessary to mark off their space with a chalk line or a strip of tape so they know exactly where the boundaries are. This approach enables a teacher to exert a reasonable amount of control over hyperactive pupils. But it will work only if the adjusted rules are strictly enforced.

It is also helpful to give these wiggly children something to play with in their hands. They almost always bring an item from home to fill this purpose, but it is usually a toy that is so much fun that it demands all their attention and keeps them and their neighbours from work. A piece of modelling clay, a big rubber band-anything they can twist and squeeze without distracting their classmates-can help them sit still and focus. For testing, a private place is almost always essential. LD/ADD students who cause constant discipline problems should also be seated in the back. With them, the teacher's objective is to protect the rest of the class from the disturbances they create. Situating these youngsters in a corner of the back row has the effect of separating them from the other children. No one has to watch their antics, and there is only one neighbour to be disturbed.

For more complete separation, a disruptive boy can be surrounded by girls who will not interact with him. He should not be given the enlarged territory allowed the hyperactive child. And he should not be placed in some remote corner that isolates him entirely. Children's preferences can be a great help in determining the ideal location and type of seating. The learning styles research of Drs. Rita and Kenneth Dunn is also useful in analysing the five environmental factors that must be considered when choosing an appropriate study locale.

*Noise*: The noise level is of primary importance. For many pupils, deep concentration is so easy that they stay engrossed in their work despite even loud sounds. Very few LD/ADD youngsters have the ability to tune out the smallest background noises. It's usually difficult-and sometimes impossible-to provide the degree of quiet they need when there are other students nearby. For those who can tolerate looking "different," sound insulating earmuffs like those used at airports may be helpful. Earplugs and stereo headsets playing white noise offer the same benefits at less expense.

Many learners actually need noise in order to concentrate. Background sounds from a radio, stereo, or television help such students filter out the intrusive background noises that would otherwise disrupt their concentration. There is a growing body of evidence to suggest that certain types of classical music can be an aid to concentration and learning. For LD/ADD students who find music helpful during study sessions, a small cassette or CD player with a headset can be extremely valuable.

*Light*: The amount of light in the work area can have a strong effect on concentration. Some students find that dim lighting makes them sleepy and sluggish, while bright light helps them stay alert. Others find that low light helps them feel calm and focused, while intense light makes them fidgety and nervous. Several studies have shown that poor readers and right brain thinkers tend to prefer dim light for study. As might be expected, many LD/ADD students find it easiest to learn in a room with low intensity lighting. Perhaps baseball hats should be allowed in classrooms as a socially acceptable form of eyeshade.

*Temperature*: Personal preferences concerning room temperature vary widely. While some students fan themselves and complain of the heat, others seated nearby shiver. There is a limited temperature range within which the human brain functions well. When the classroom thermometer registers above eighty degrees, the mind becomes sleepy and sluggish; when the reading falls below the mid-sixties, discomfort disrupts serious thinking. Youngsters with a learning disability and/or an attention deficit disorder seem especially susceptible to extremes of cold or heat. Consequently, the teacher's personal comfort level shouldn't dictate what's right for an entire classroom. Students need to be taught to adjust their clothing according to the temperature so they can remain clear-headed and alert. It is essential that classroom temperature be monitored closely.

*Seating*: Standard classroom seating isn't ideal for all pupils. Mozart wrote his music standing up at a high table. Others do their best thinking stretched out on the floor. Some can't concentrate unless they're in motion. While it's more convenient for the teacher to have the entire class sitting in chairs lined up in neat rows, LD/ ADD students should be encouraged to explore alternate postures.

– Oral stimulation: Many people find that the machinery of thinking works best when accompanied by movements of the mouth. When concentrating, they chew on a pencil, smoke a pipe, eat, drink, chew gum, or bite their fingernails. Some experts believe that such activity "integrates" the nervous system. Although food and drink aren't normally available in a classroom, many youngsters with a learning disability and/or an attention deficit disorder could benefit from such intake.

Some very small adjustments in the classroom environment can make a gigantic difference in a student's academic achievement. Always, in selecting the ideal seat for an LD/ADD student, the teacher needs to look for a quiet spot with little traffic, a limited view, and few neighbours. The neighbours can be as important as the location. A youngster with a learning disability and/ or an attention deficit disorder should not be seated near children who pick on him or tease him. Talkative students and those who fool around a lot should also be avoided. The LD/ADD child's distractibility is bothersome enough without noisy classmates nearby to make it worse. A seat beside a pleasant, quiet, good student can have a very steadying effect.

## Choosing Right Neighbour

By choosing the right neighbour and carefully controlling an adjusted set of rules, the teacher can see to it that pupils with a learning disability and/or an attention deficit disorder have a ready source of information available right there at their elbow. The teacher, the LD/ADD child, and the neighbour must all have a clear understanding of the special arrangements they're making to create a "good neighbour plan."

1. The two youngsters are allowed to talk openly and freely but quietly during class.

2. The LD/ADD student is not permitted to pester his neighbour or use the conversations as an excuse for socializing.

3. The "good neighbour" must maintain a cooperative, understanding attitude.

4. To make sure that the children understand the difference between a "good neighbour plan" and a partnership, the teacher must establish clear and specific guidelines. The youngsters must know what kinds of questions the LD/ ADD student may take to his neighbour. "What does this word say?" or "Do the answers have to be in sentences?" would probably be allowed. "What's the answer to this question?" would definitely not be acceptable.

   The two children also have to understand exactly what kind of help the neighbour may provide. Is he to copy arithmetic problems from the book? Does he supply answers to basic questions such as "How much is 14 take away 6?" Is he responsible for reminding the LD/ ADD child about capital letters and punctuation? There must also be a clear understanding of special situations when their talking will not be allowed. Does the policy remain in effect during tests? Does it apply only in one classroom or anywhere in the school?

Most LD/ADD students ask two questions repeatedly: "What's that word?" and "How do you spell ?" They need to know where to turn for answers to these questions no matter what the situation. Most difficulties can be avoided if the full details are settled at the time the agreement is made. By the fifth grade, Mike had overcome almost all of the problems caused by his learning disability. In most areas, he was a good student. He was especially patient with himself about his poor spelling.

Whenever he got stuck on a word, he went quietly to the teacher to ask for help. But Mike did not deal with his copying problem so effectively. Copying things off the blackboard caused him serious difficulties. Every time he made a mistake, he got terribly upset. Erasing and correcting his errors made him furious. It got to the point where Mike caused at least one ugly scene every day. In mid-November, a new boy, Tim, enrolled in the class. For no particular reason, the teacher gave him a seat next to Mike.

## Time Limits

Many children with a learning disability and/or an attention deficit disorder race through life at high velocity; they are hyperactive. Some slow moving LD/ADD youngsters are referred to as hypoactive. Regardless of LD/ADD students' preferred pace, time tends to slip through their fingers. Whenever they're allowed out of the classroom, it's unlikely they'll be seen again soon. A two-minute trip to the bathroom takes them five minutes-or often fifteen. For a short errand to the office or library, they'll be gone twice as long as seems reasonable. Much of this is to be expected and tolerated, but a few tricks can help. Many teachers impose a time limit on students who leave the classroom for a trip to the lavatory, their locker, the drinking fountain, and so on. This is usually done with a sign-out sheet on which students record their name and the time they left the room.

Since most LD/ADD children (of all ages) have a poor concept of time, this standard method doesn't always work for them. They seem to have no internal "feel" for time. With no mental clock to pressure them to move along, they use up the allotted time on a sightseeing trip through the halls. Those who have a watch and are willing to use it rarely have any skill at figuring out what time it will be when their time is up. More than their classmates, LD/ADD students need something to force them to hurry along on their errands. The sign-out approach can work for an LD/ADD student if he uses an hourglass, a cooking timer, or a stopwatch instead of a clock. When leaving the room, the student takes the hourglass or timer from a shelf near the door, starts it running, and places it on his own desk. If he returns before the sand runs out or the bell goes off, he merely puts it back on its shelf and returns to his seat. If he's late, he suffers some standard penalty.

With all types of students in grades one through twelve, this method gives the teacher a way to enforce rules governing how long pupils are allowed out of the classroom. It has two distinct advantages: it's no trouble to the teacher at all, and it does not single out LD/ ADD children for special treatment. The time limits apply equally to all. For those youngsters who are repeatedly late with the timer, some other system must be devised. A sturdy nametag (giving address and phone number for both home and school) is a necessity for young LD/ADD children being taken off the school grounds.

A buddy system can also be effective in such situations. It is not wise to let LD/ADD youths be the last one in line at any time. If not kept under a watchful eye, the quick ones dart off to explore, while the slow ones become engrossed in something and stop entirely. As part of their nonvariable pace, most LD/ADD youngsters have trouble shifting from one activity to another. "It's time for music." "Turn in your sentences and get out your dictionary." "Put away your math and go wash for lunch." The school day is full of abrupt changes. Some students develop a habit of pleading, "I'm not done yet." Others just ignore the requested action.

LD/ADD students are particularly prone to causing trouble when concluding one activity and beginning another. In the first place, they frequently fail to complete their work within the period allotted. Also, their faulty concept of time makes it difficult for them to gauge how many minutes they have left for a particular activity. For them, the order to turn in their paper comes as a total surprise. No mental timer has made them aware of the looming deadline. If LD/ADD youngsters are not mentally prepared, they balk. Instead of making an agreeable, efficient change from math to reading, they keep right on with math, or begin horsing around, or stare off into space. Orders that come like a bolt out of the blue simply do not produce the desired responses. The regular use of a five minute warning can work wonders.

Within the classroom, a simple "Five minutes left for the health project" can help the entire class get into the right frame of mind for the coming change. On the playground or in the lunchroom, the teacher can signal by holding up five fingers. Even homeschoolers have to deal with activity shifts and need to give advance notice to set the stage. Then, when the moment for the change arrives, everyone knows the time for action is now. No excuses are accepted. The five-minute warning makes it possible for a teacher to impose the added structure needed to get LD/ ADD youngsters to live within some kind of schedule.

## Organisation Skills

The school day is a procession of varied activities requiring frequent transitions which pose no problem for most students. For LD/ADD children, each task shift provides a new opportunity for the mind to drift. Long after the new assignment has been given and the rest of the class has settled down to work, students with a learning disability and/or an attention deficit disorder can be found staring off into space-without ever having gotten out the necessary materials. It isn't a matter of not doing good work. If left to their own devices, LD/ADD students don't do any work. They never get started. Traditional methods of dealing with this difficulty can stimulate the child to action, but they rarely keep the situation from recurring. Instead of undergoing a lasting change of behaviour, the child learns to wait for others to force him into motion.

He doesn't learn techniques for self-monitoring and self-discipline. He has little chance to develop organizational skills, initiative, and independence. Both student and teacher are damaged by continual conflict The teacher's patient optimism wilts, while the youngster comes to view authority figures as enemies. Standard corrective measures can make matters worse. Many of them deprive the student of an opportunity for real success with the work assigned. Removing the child from the classroom can solve the problem, provided that the alternate location is quiet and well supervised. But that is rarely the case in the cloakrooms, corridors, back corners, and office spaces that are readily available in today's schools.

Sometimes, in an attempt to force a pupil to get his work done, teachers unintentionally reward him for being unproductive in the normal setting. Teachers should abandon any efficiency enhancing techniques that allow the youngster to get out of doing his work and have a great time while he's not doing it. Truly effective solutions come from recognizing the root of the problem and making adjustments there. LD/ADD children are dreamers. That can't be changed. But it is possible to avoid or alter situations that send them off into the clouds.

A child with a learning disability and/or an attention deficit disorder almost always has trouble shifting gears and getting started on a new activity. A large part of this difficulty can be attributed to the fact that he is so disorganized. He doesn't get his book out because he can't find it. Or in the process of looking for it, he discovers some long-forgotten treasure buried at the bottom of his desk. Every time an LD/ADD youngster looks into his desk or locker, he takes a trip to never-never land. Many problems can be solved by simply keeping the student out of his desk and his locker. His rummaging time can be limited to a five-minute period first thing every morning. Within that time, he must get out everything needed for the entire day. A schedule and a list of daily supplies should be taped close at hand for easy reference. For some LD/ADD children, a materials partner is necessary to help with the process of "getting it together" for the day.

While an LD/ADD child is learning to get control of time and supplies, it is sometimes best to have him keep all books, notebooks, and equipment on an open shelf or in a cabinet within easy reach. This eliminates the need for (and breaks the habit of) desk digging entirely. In extreme cases, a teacher can keep custody of all his materials. That sounds impractical, but it's actually more efficient than the repeated confrontations that develop when disorganization becomes a chronic problem for a student.

Smart teachers do not allow a child with a learning disability and/or an attention deficit disorder to take textbooks out of the classroom. It is also wise to monitor the LD/ ADD student's inventory of school supplies on a regular basis so that pencil and paper are always available for use in class. Ideally, the pupil provides these materials and always has them with him. Even with careful control, a backup system will be necessary. An old coffee can full of pencil stubs will usually suffice for emergency needs. No matter what measures have to be taken, make sure an LD/ ADD youngster never has to leave the room to go in search of supplies. Sight-seeing trips around the building take much more time than can be allowed.

Notebooks are a special source of difficulty. Unless some kind of system is forced upon them, LD/ADD students do their English assignment in their science notebook, leave worksheets at home on the kitchen table, and never have what they need with them in class. A notebook control system is absolutely essential if these disorganized youngsters are going to have the faintest hope of being properly prepared for class.

A teacher can use it without the help of parents. The family can set it up without involving the school. Either way, it takes at least six weeks of close monitoring to help the student develop the habit of using the system. During this break-in period, the entire binder must be checked daily, night and morning. At this time, missing items should be replaced, inaccurate notations corrected, and important messages made current.

Checks on a calendar in connection with some system of rewards can supply the motivation needed to get the student cooperatively involved. It also helps if the youngster adds personal touches in accord with his own tastes and interests. Stickers, artwork, monograms, and slogans can convert a distasteful form of discipline into a source of personal pride. Be sure every piece of the binder is clearly labelled with the student's name, address, phone number, school, teacher's name, and grade. If misplaced, easily identified materials are likely to be returned.

Many LD/ADD students are highly resistant to setting up such a materials control system, yet they are the very ones who need it the most. If it is imposed by the authority in charge, designed by the youngster, and monitored closely with an enforcement system based on positive rewards, it leads almost all students to develop the desired organizational habits within six to eight weeks. With those few truly scatter-brained youngsters who are totally unable to develop orderly habits, teachers have to monitor the system for the entire year. That sounds like a lot of work - until the alternatives are considered. If active supervision is not available for the first few weeks of this materials control system, it should not be started. This programme can produce the desired behaviour change only if the student is provided with the necessary materials and is systematically taught how to use them.

## Controlling Distractions

Modern electronic equipment offers some amazing alternatives in controlling the distractions in the LD/ADD student's learning environment. Through the use of a headset, the auditory level of a student's environment can be almost completely controlled. Distracting noises in the classroom can be masked by neutral, nondisturbing sound. Although many types of music produce the masking effect, research has shown that classical music, particularly Bach, actually enhances the brain's processing capacity. When selecting the music for a classroom Walkman or portable CD player, it's not a matter of matching the student's personal taste; the goal is to find the music that does the best job of building concentration.

Computers offer an even more powerful aid to overcoming distractibility and short attention span. Since they are so visually stimulating and offer tactile and kinesthetic involvement, they can rivet a student's attention to the screen and get him immersed in instruction. Youngsters with a learning disability and/or an attention deficit disorder often have a strong talent for computers. The languages and methods of processing make sense to them in world of written language does not. For many LD/ADD pupils, sitting down to mouse or keyboard triggers the "hyperfocus" mechanisms that make them get totally absorbed in whatever activity is on the screen. Since it produces a state that is the extreme opposite of their usual classroom distractibility, it can be helpful in all academic areas.

## Social Problems

Any student who takes more than his fair share of the teacher's time any pupil who ruins the peaceful atmosphere of the classroom with strange or disruptive behaviour any child who gets away with ignoring rules, schedules, and assignments any youngster who keeps the entire classroom in turmoil is resented and rejected by his classmates. Thus, prevention must be the teacher's first line of defence against the LD/ADD child's social problems. Through careful classroom management and all the special adjustments, the teacher must help children with a learning disability and/

or an attention deficit disorder succeed with their schoolwork.

If they can do their math, they won't have the tantrums that make other children think they're weird. If they can finish their assignment on time, the others won't grow restless and angry because they're constantly being kept waiting for this one slow worker. Everything that makes it possible for LD/ADD students to function satisfactorily within the classroom makes them more acceptable to their classmates.

While using this indirect approach to achieve long-range goals, teachers need to be on guard against issues that require firm, direct intervention. "I don't want to sit next to her." "I don't want him on my team." "Does he have to be on our committee?" Statements like these hurt, but LD/ADD youngsters often feel a stronger level of rejection than is intended. As long as there is no name-calling or open ridicule, the issue is best treated as a social snub. For the offender, the routine lecture that a classroom is not a social club is appropriate. Then the matter should be dropped.

Rejection that includes name-calling and cruel teasing needs to be treated as a major offence. Just as a teacher does not allow anyone to use ethnic slurs in referring to minorities," she must not tolerate children calling an LD/ADD child "stupid" or "retard." Such name-calling calls for strong, immediate corrective action. Teachers need to keep in mind that children mirror the attitudes and behaviour of the adults around them.

Any person who does not recognize the talents as well as the weaknesses that make the LD/ADD child different will find it difficult to be supportive. The classroom teacher involved with a student who has a learning disability and/

or an attention deficit disorder is faced with a three-step process: first, she must learn to understand and accept the child; then she must develop strong positive expectations of success for the youngster; and finally, she must lead the class to do the same. The key is in developing a firm belief that this child, too, can grow into a happy, productive adult.

The many important functions that underlie learning are not always measurable on traditional tests used to diagnose learning problems. However, through a teacher's careful analyses of task and performance expectations, it is possible to determine which functions are required for the mastery of skills and content at each grade level. There is also a range of behaviour expectations that can be observed when the student interacts with the teacher, the curriculum, and other students in the classroom. By observing these behaviours and carefully analysing performance expectations, it is possible for teachers to determine individual patterns of strengths and weaknesses.

Teachers can also observe where breakdowns in the learning process are occurring. A well-trained teacher, with keen observation skills and knowledge of neuro developmental functions and associated behaviours, has the best opportunity to search for and identify learning strengths and weaknesses. Teachers may find recurrent themes indicative of student performance patterns

- in the classroom environment
- in the context (content and format) of the curriculum materials
- in the work demands of the tasks the student is being asked to perform (volume, memory, organization, and rate)

- Parents, too, have the opportunity to make such observations and provide additional important information.

The key to thorough knowledge of student learning abilities is not in the quantity of right and wrong answers. Instead, knowing a student's strengths and weaknesses and identifying breakdowns in the learning process come from direct, systematic, and sensitive observation of

- patterns of errors and successes from multiple sources and samples
- how the student performs tasks
- when and in what context successes and difficulties occur
- with what consistency the behaviours occur
- the ease, fluency, and capacity in assimilating and expressing new knowledge
- affective reactions and coping strategies

By observing and searching for recurrent themes, a management plan for every student can be achieved. These plans will enhance learning, reduce frustration, and provide success—necessities for the maintenance of self-esteem and learning motivation. Well designed plans

- help students understand themselves
- guarantee protection against public humiliation
- foster self-esteem and pride
- preserve a student's personal accountability
- facilitate the strengthening of strengths and affinities
- accommodate or bypass impeding dysfunctions and skill deficits

- include direct interventions at the breakdown points, so as to strive to improve weak
- functions and skills
- enlist collaboration between teachers, students, and parents

A teacher's observations are a powerful tool for turning student failure into success through well-designed interventions.

### *Group and Grouping Retellings*

Providing a means of including struggling learners in classroom activities is a problem facing teachers at all grade levels. 'Sruggling learners" means any students functioning at two or more levels below current grade placement. These students may or may not be served by a resource room teacher in reading or special education. They come to the attention of teachers because they are experiencing difficulty keeping up with assignments both in and outside the classroom. Eventually, as they grow older and their frustration increases, such students often give up and drop out of school, either literally or figuratively.

Consequently, it is imperative that we find ways to include the struggling learner in the classroom community. One approach that has promise is the use of flexible grouping strategies inherent in collaborative learning, which, according to a number of studies, improves everything from achievement to self-esteem. Before using group retellings, it is necessary to organize students into heterogeneous 4-student groups. One way to achieve this is to use "buddy system" groups. Determine buddy groups by first ranking the class from "most prepared" to "least prepared"' for the subject matter (e.g., number the students from I to 30). Next, divide them into 3 subgroups, so that the groups resemble the traditional high, middle, and low ability groups. Finally, achieve heterogeneous grouping by assigning the top student in each of the three groups to one group, the second-highest student in each to another, the third-highest to another, and so forth.

You will then have students 1, 11, and 21 in one group; students 2, 12, and 22 in another; and so on, with the last group consisting of students 10, 20, and 30. In this way, the mixed groups should comprise individuals who are sufficiently different in ability that they can benefit from each other's help, but not so different that they find one another intimidating. Inform the students of their group assignments, and tell them that they are buddies and must help each other as needed, whether by reading each other's work before it is turned in, by answering questions regarding assignments, by showing a partner how to do something, or by discussing a story and sharing their recollections. In addition, let them know that this is only one of many grouping arrangements that you will be using.

Whether you choose to use the buddy system just described or some other form of heterogeneous grouping, you are now ready to engage the students in group retellings.

1. Tell the students to read a portion of their text, either silently or by whispering in pairs. Then, instead of asking the commercially prepared questions that teacher's manuals provide, have the students tell their partners and group members what they remember about the text.

2. If students are unaccustomed to group retelling, you may want to "tell aloud" your own retelling of a brief selection to model your expectations for the students.

Be sure to include analogies, personal anecdotes, and imagery to embellish your retelling. Tell the students that by personalizing their reading, they help to enhance their later recall of the content.

3. Be sure to circulate among the groups to "eavesdrop" on their conversations, to assist when needed, and to ask probing questions to further their discussions.
4. After the reading and retelling sessions, elicit responses from the class about what they have read. You can do so after they read each segment, or after they complete the entire selection, depending on the overall ability level of the class.
5. Write the students' responses on the board or on an overhead transparency so that they are clearly visible to everyone.

The group retelling strategy is beneficial in many ways. First, it maximizes class participation and gives everyone a chance to engage in the learning process. Second, students read the information, engage in a group discussion, contribute their recollections and then see the content again in print on the board. They thus experience the content in many different modalities using the language of their peers, not just the stilted language of the textbook. The resulting lesson is far different from the typical assignment to read the entire chapter and answer the questions at the end-a task that is often overwhelming for the struggling learner.

Students who have difficulty with the initial reading of the selection may gather some of their group contributions from pictures, charts, or specific words or concepts in the text. Other options include giving struggling learners in each group topically related alternative material that is written on an easier level. Speaking in front of a small group is less threatening than being called on to answer a question in the presence of the entire class. Students also find that their own associations are triggered when they hear others in the group remember a fact or event. The benefits of using group or paired retellings are not limited to reading assignments alone. Students also can profit from retellings after they watch a video, observe an experiment, listen to an outside speaker or go on a field trip.

### Cooperative Learning Strategies

The social studies teacher surveys her class as students work on a cooperative learning activity. Shane consults his strategy card, looks at the instructions on the board, and returns to work. The teacher is pleased as she observes that the students with learning disabilities are more actively involved than before. Increased participation is the result of instructing students to use a preprinted strategy card to self-monitor participation in mainstream, cooperative learning activities. Using the learning strategy model proposed by Deschler and Schumaker, we developed an instructional procedure that employed preprinted 3 x 5 index cards and an accompanying script. We designed these cards to assist students to appropriately seek clarification on the expectations of the assignment and to focus on the group activity.

Throughout the lesson, students self-monitor for attention by asking themselves if they are listening and participating. At the completion of the activity, students use a comprehension self-check by asking themselves what they learned during the lesson. This instructional approach is designed for intermediate through secondary grades. Teachers could modify the procedure for younger students, however, by using symbols to represent each step; or the exact wording could be adapted for individual students.

For learning and generalization to occur, students with learning disabilities should receive the instruction and practice in at least two settings (e.g., resource room and mainstreamed classroom). Initially, the special education teacher introduces the strategy cards by reading the designated script. Students then practice the technique in small groups in the resource room. When these students seem to be competent in using the procedure, the mainstream teacher then presents the strategy to the entire class. This instruction is followed immediately by a cooperative learning activity in which all students practice the new strategy.

## USE OF TEACHING STRATEGIES

### *Step 1: Introduction*

Begin by saying:

> In many of your classes, teachers ask students to work in small groups to do learning activities. Sometimes, students get confused about what to do during those activities. Here are some cards that may help you work in these small groups.

Hand the preprinted cards to the students and explain:

> This card may help you know what to do in these activities. You can carry it to class with you as a reminder of what to think about at those times.

Pointing to the top of the card, say:

> The top of the card tells what students do in group activities. Let's read it together: "When 10 am in a group activity, I work with group members to discuss information, solve problems, or work on a project. " There are three underlined words. What are they?

That's right, discuss, solve, and work. This tells you when you are in a group activity, you might discuss or talk about a topic, such as things we do to harm the environment; you might solve a problem, like figuring out what to take with you on a trip to the moon; or you might work on a project, such as preparing a report for the class on recent changes in Russia.

Let's read the next sentence, "I am a valuable member of the group." Sometimes members of a group feel they have nothing to share. This sentence on your card is a reminder that you are important to your group. Each time you begin a group activity, read these two sentences to remind yourself of what you might be doing and that you are an important group member.

### *Step 2: Understanding*

Show students how to use the cards to increase their understanding of the task at hand:

> Let's read number 1 together: "Before beginning, I ask myself: Do I understand the directions and goal of the group activity?" This means that you should try to say to yourself what the group is expected to do during the activity.
>
> Let's read number 2. "If I do not understand the directions or goal of the activity, I ask the group members. If they do not know, I may then ask the teacher to explain the directions or goal again." It is important that you make sure you understand what you are supposed to do. If you do not understand the directions, first ask members of your group because one of the purposes of a group activity is to learn to work with fellow students. Then, if no one in your group is clear about the directions, ask the teacher. Who do you ask first if you don't understand the

> directions? [Students reply: "Group members."] Yes, that's right, group members.

### *Step 3: Reminders*

Show students how to use the self-questions on the card to remind themselves to listen and to make contributions to the group activity:

> Let's read number 3 together: "Every few minutes, I ask myself: Am I listening to the group members? Am I helping in some way to complete the group activity?" This is a reminder to listen to the students who are talking. This is also a reminder to participate in the group. You will get more out of these activities if you will remind yourself every few minutes to listen and participate.

### *Step 4: Learning*

Show students how to use the card to monitor their own learning while they are participating in cooperative learning groups:

> Let's read number 4 together: "At the end of the activity, I complete this sentence: I learned that. . . " When you are finished with a group activity, you should have learned something. One way to check your understanding is to take a moment to tell yourself something you learned . When would you use this card ?

# 3

# ICTs in Teacher Education

A vision for ICTs in Education often precedes the development of standards. Many regions and countries in Europe, the USA, Asia, and Australia have adopted a set of ICT standards for pre-service and in-service teacher education. One illustrative example is the Singapore government's Master Plan for Information Technology (IT) in Education, launched in 1997 to usher in a new era of educational development. It specified three goals:

- To train every teacher in purposeful use of IT for teaching;
- To equip teachers with core skills in teaching with IT; and
- To involve institutions of higher education and industry partners in schools.

In Singapore, the National Institute for Education (NIE) is the only provider of pre-service teacher education. In her review of pre-service teacher training in ICTs, Jung describes keys to the success of ICTs integration. NIE's approach includes several notable strategies.

- It provides a short foundation course that focuses on hands-on IT experience as the initial stage of pre-service training.
- It provides more advanced IT courses as electives for students who need or want to develop more advanced IT-based pedagogical skills.
- It integrates IT components into all of the subject matter areas such as math, social studies, English, and so on, so that students have a rolemodel for IT-integrated teaching and learning.
- It designs IT-integrated courses in such a way that students have the opportunity to produce IT-based instructional materials themselves and share outcomes of the course with others.

## Implementation of ICT's in Teacher Education

This section describes a set of standards developed in the USA and contrasts it with approaches in other countries, particularly within Europe. The International Society for Technology in Education (ISTE) has developed a set of standards to provide guidance and consistency to programmes. These standards are used widely in several countries and serve as the National Educational Technology Standards (NETS) for the United States of America.

The ISTE NETS for Students (NETS*S) describe what students from pre-school to grade twelve should know about and be able to do with technology. The student standards provide a basis for the development of technology standards for teachers and technology standards for educational administrators. These sets of standards provide states, districts, schools, and teacher education institutions the foundations upon which the integration of technology in their programmes can be built. Other countries and regions that have developed, adopted, or adapted national or regional standards include: Australia, China, Ireland, Latin America and the United Kingdom.

Whether a university is establishing a new teacher education programme specialising in ICT leadership or redesigning an existing teacher education programme into which technology is to be woven, ICT standards can provide a substantial foundation for the planning process. For example, the ISTE NETS for Teachers can provide guidance in the planning process for addressing all four of the major components in the Framework for ICTs in Teacher Education. ISTE's performance-based standards describe what the teacher candidates should do to demonstrate that they are competent users of ICTs and that they can facilitate competent use of technology by their students.

The ISTE National Educational Technology Standards for Teachers, provides standards and performance indicators describing what pre-service teachers should know about and be able to do with technology upon completion of their teacher preparation programme. The four key components providing the framework for technology competence can be supported through implementation of the six ISTE standards.

Standard I addresses technical competence. Standards II, III, and IV address preparation, implementation, and assessment supporting content learning, effective pedagogical strategies, and informative performance assessment practices. Standard V speaks to the use of ICT tools for a variety of professional, communication, and collaborative activities among teachers. Standard VI addresses the social, ethical, legal, and human issues inherent when technology expands communications and learning opportunities globally. The rapid infusion of technology into schools requires a new generation of leaders who are able to use the new tools to enhance their own productivity and decision-making activities and who understand the importance of integrating technology into the learning process.

Leadership is often the most important factor in the successful integration of ICTs into the school's instructional practices and curriculum. Research has shown that without effective and supportive leadership, changes in the teaching-learning process and widespread, effective uses of technology in learning are not likely to occur. To encourage educators to prepare for positions of leadership in ICTs, the ISTE Accreditation and Professional Standards Committee has developed accreditation standards for teacher preparation programmes for specialisation in ICTs.

The technology specialisation guidelines have been adopted by the National Council for Accreditation of Teacher Education (NCATE) and are currently used in evaluation of teacher preparation programmes for accreditation. Reprinted with permission from National Educational Technology Standards for Teachers, published by the International Society for Technology in Education. NETS Project, copyright 2000, ISTE. (http://cnets.iste.org). All rights reserved. ISTE/NCATE accreditation standards for programmes in educational computing and technology include:

- ISTE/NCATE Standards for Educational Computing and Technology Facilitationinitial endorsement programme to prepare technology literacy teachers or campus leaders who support teachers' integration of technology in the classrooms;

- ISTE/NCATE Standards for Educational Computing and Technology Leadership-advanced programme to prepare district, state, or regional educational technology coordinators; and
- ISTE/NCATE Educational Computing and Technology Secondary Computer Science Education Standards-initial endorsement or degree programmes to prepare secondary teachers of computer science.

The documented importance of a shared vision among the multiple levels of an organisation indicates the need for technology standards for education administrators. ISTE managed the development of Technology Standards for School Administrators (TSSA), which identify performance standards for the technology skills, knowledge, and dispositions of education administrators.

The TSSA Collaborative has developed standards for school administrators that include specific indicators for the superintendent, school administrator, and district level administrator. School administrators must understand and support the use of technology at all levels so that they can work collaboratively with universities on appropriate field placements and help new teachers incorporate technology into classroom instruction.

Many countries in Europe have official recommendations for ICT-related skills for future and practicing teachers. Eurydice, the information network on education in Europe, annually publishes Basic Indicators on the Incorporation of ICT into European Education Systems. Some countries state only that teaching about ICTs is compulsory, without specifying what skills should be developed and what content should be included. In the majority of European countries, as much importance is attached to the teachers' personal command of ICTs as to mastery of ICTs for teaching purposes. Recommended most frequently in lower secondary education are the use of word processing and data processing software.

In France, the Netherlands and the United Kingdom, the content of training is determined to some extent by the mandatory standards. In the UK, there is also a detailed curriculum for the use of ICTs in teaching specific subjects. Countries and regions adopting standards for the first time may wish to do so in stages. This was the strategy taken by the UK, which currently has the most detailed standards of any country in Europe. The standards were first imposed with a relatively simple section within the mandatory standards (criteria for government approval of courses) for pre-service teachers in 1989. This section states:

On completion of their course, all students should be able to select and make appropriate use of a range of equipment and resources to promote learning. In particular, all courses should contain compulsory and clearly identifiable elements that enable students to make effective use of information technology (IT) in the classroom and provide a sound basis for their subsequent development in the field. They should be trained to:

- make confident personal use of a range of software packages and IT devices appropriate to their subject specialisation and age range;
- review critically the relevance of software packages and IT devices to their subject specialisation and age range and judge the potential value of these in classroom use;
- make constructive use of IT in their teaching and in particular prepare and put into effect schemes of work incorporating appropriate uses of IT; and

- evaluate the ways in which the use of IT changes the nature of teaching and learning.

  Some years later the UK government developed highly detailed standards for pre-service teacher education and then also developed a nation-wide strategy to train all teachers in pedagogical use of ICTs. The detailed curriculum has the following expected outcomes for teachers. Teachers should know:

- when, when not and how to use ICTs in teaching their subject;
- how ICTs can be used for teaching the whole class;
- how ICTs can be used when planning, including the use of ICTs for lesson preparation and the choice and organisation of ICT resources;
- how to assess pupils' work when ICTs have been used; and
- how ICTs can be used to keep up-to-date, share best practice and reduce bureaucracy.

Each competency has between 0 and 8 statements. The complete curriculum is available online. The Teacher Training Agency also developed a CD to help teachers analyse their own training needs. A complementary outcomes-based curriculum has also been developed for school librarians. An ICT training initiative funded by a charitable lottery has resulted in the creation of a large number of training organisations, many of which are public-private partnerships. The largest of these is the partnership between the Open University School of Education and Research Machines Ltd.

A different approach has been taken in Scandinavia. A standard test was first developed that focused on ICT skills.

It is known as the European Computer Driving License (ECDL) and is used in many professions and with students in schools. More recently, a Pedagogical ICT Driving License (the Paedagogisk IT-kørekort) has been developed for primary and secondary school teachers in Denmark for the integration of ICTs in education. It is organised into modules that teachers study in small groups, preferably with teachers in the same school working on a coherent plan under the guidance of a distant tutor.

Several countries in South America have extensive projects to develop and integrate ICTs in education, but the lack of national policies for the use of ICTs is notable. The Enlaces project in Chile, represents an exemplary national approach. SRI provided an international independent review of this initiative called World Links for Development. The project recommended the following for Brazil:

- Articulation and dissemination of a vision of how ICTs fit into the broader society and education. Together policy-makers and educators can build a strong national policy that clearly outlines how ICTs advance national goals and promote innovation use of ICTs to improve teaching and learning.
- Emphasize technology integration and interdisciplinary collaborative projects as the main topics for teacher training, and tie ICTs use to the development of basic skills in students.

These recommendations fit well with the Framework illustrated and with projects in Europe that have curriculum approaches that build teamwork among teachers within and among schools.

The final example provided is the generic curriculum used by the internationalIntel Applying Computers in Education (ACE) project. The project trains classroom teachers to integrate the use of computers into existing curriculum to increase student learning and achievement. Originated in the USA in 1998, it is now in operation in several countries. The curriculum is summarised by these themes of training:

– Using computers and learning and productivity tools for both teachers and students.

- Using the types of computers and software that are widely available in both schools and industry.

– An emphasis on "hands-on" learning and the creation of lessons which teachers can effectively use in their classrooms.

- Encouraging teachers to work in teams, problem-solve and participate in peer-review of their lessons.

### *ICT Curriculum*

A first step in determining the ICT curriculum for a university teacher education programme is to examine the expectations identified in the ICT standards for students, or standards for teachers aligned with the student standards. Through the ongoing use of technology in the schooling process, students should achieve important technology capabilities. The key individual in helping students achieve those capabilities is the classroom teacher. The teacher is responsible for establishing the classroom environment and preparing the learning opportunities that facilitate students' use of technology to learn, communicate, and develop knowledge products; consequently, it is critical that all classroom teachers are prepared to provide their students with these opportunities. Teacher preparation programmes must provide technology-rich experiences throughout all aspects of the training programmes.

Teachers must be prepared to empower students with the advantages technology can bring. Schools and classrooms, both real and virtual, must have teachers who are equipped with technology resources and skills and who can effectively teach the necessary subject matter content while incorporating technology concepts and skills. Real-world connections, primary source materials, and sophisticated data-gathering and analysis tools are only a few of the resources that allow teachers to provide heretofore unimaginable opportunities for developing their students' conceptual understandings.

Traditional educational practices no longer provide pre-service teachers with the skills necessary to teach students to survive economically in today's workplace. Teachers must prepare their students to apply strategies for problem solving, and to use appropriate tools for learning, calculating, collaborating, and communicating. ICT tools and resources can contribute dramatically to establishing these new learning environments, both in P-12 schools and in colleges of education.

Teacher educators must therefore model the use of these new learning environments in their own university classrooms. The curriculum for teacher educators is often rich with strategies for presenting subject matter and pedagogy; however, it may be lean in terms of integrating technological tools for supporting that learning. Consequently, curriculum developers for teacher preparation programmes must be vigilant in identifying appropriate ways to apply ICT tools throughout the coursework and experiences planned for pre-service teachers.

### *Model Strategies for Intergrating ICTs*

In an effort to implement ICT standards in a variety of coursework taken by preservice teachers across all subject disciplines, a number of methods and strategies have been identified. Many of these strategies employ commonly used productivity tools such as word processing, database, spreadsheet, or browser applications. These software tools can be used in countless ways to support the subject area curricula. Additional strategies, that are multipurpose in application, may also be used to help teacher candidates quickly develop technology-rich lessons for their fieldwork.

### *Web-Based Lessons*

#### *WebQuests*

A WebQuest is an inquiry-oriented activity in which most or all of the information used by learners is drawn from the Web. WebQuests are designed to use learners' time well, to focus on using information rather than looking for it, and to support learners' thinking at the levels of analysis, synthesis, and evaluation. The WebQuest model has been effectively applied to all levels of education, from elementary to postgraduate study, and in many different subject Areas. The WebQuest provides teachers an option of reviewing and selecting web-based learning activities in a lessontype format.

The WebQuest model encourages teachers to create for their students new activities and adapt successful ones to take advantage of the Web's power. A higher-level application of this model has students develop their own Web-Quest activities to support the subject matter they are studying, and share the WebQuests with their peers.

### *CyberGuides*

CyberGuides include standards-based, web-delivered units of instruction centred on core works of literature. CyberGuides provide a quick supplementary set of activities for students (and pre-service teachers) as they explore specific pieces of literature. Each CyberGuide contains a student and teacher edition, targeted standards, a description of the task, a process by which the task may be completed, teacher-selected web sites, and an assessment rubric. The teacher's guide includes an overview of the activities, suggestions from the author, and a library of links. The student guides include activity directions written in a format appropriate for the age and reading ability of the students. One example of a CyberGuide unit (for the intermediate grades) is "Dragonwings" by Laurence Yep

### ***Multimedia Presentations***

Multimedia combines media objects such as text, graphics, video, animation, and sound to represent and convey information. In this project-based method of teaching and learning, students acquire new knowledge and skills by designing, planning, and producing a multimedia product. Many teachers find that students are motivated to learn when they can use technology to present the results of a rich project or activity.

The multimedia presentation contains content conveyed by the student's selection of media. The teachers in training can look at examples of projects and lessons, at Internet sites housing collections of student samples. Some examples of multimedia presentations include:

– creating a web page or site;

– developing a branching hypermedia stack;

- using a multimedia slide show application to create a computer presentation;
- shooting and editing video to create a computer-generated movie.

As new forms of multimedia are explored, the types of projects become more complex. Multimedia-authoring tools are used to link and branch screens, making them interactive and layered with information in photos, scanned images, movies, and text. Students and candidates can easily narrate their projects using a microphone.

### *Telecomputing Projects*

Telecomputing projects are Internet-enriched learning activities that often involve students in one location collaborating with students or adults in one or more other locations. They may share, among other things:

- experiences
- beliefs
- data
- information
- problem-solving strategies
- products they have developed or jointly developed.

Telecomputing tools include email, electronic mailing lists, electronic bulletin boards, discussion groups, web browsers, real-time chatting, and audio- and video-conferencing. Online resources include web sites, interactive environments, and remotely operated robotic devices. Judi Harris provides a variety of telecomputing project web pages.

### Online Discussion

A common type of telecomputing activity is online discussion. With the growth of infrastructure around the world comes the ability to access others through remote connections. Students and teacher candidates can connect to experts and peers through a variety of formats, such as chat rooms, electronic bulletin boards, and email. Communicating online offers participants freedom to send and receive information efficiently across diverse geographic locations.

Communication can occur asynchronously allowing time for reflection, or to compensate for varying time zones. In real-time online communication, as in chat groups, the communication is synchronous and provides immediate feedback for reinforcement and understanding. Examples of online environments include email lists and virtual meeting places such as Tapped In. Tools such as Blackboard and WebCT may be used to create online environments.

Particular care should be taken when planning these activities across cultures and languages. Online discussions can provide rich learning experiences as the inter-cultural exchanges develop both linguistic skills and cultural knowledge. One successful strategy is for students to read in the target language, while writing in their native language. The Three Pomegranate Network of Armenian provides an excellent example of connecting a society in Diaspora-almost two thirds of Armenians live outside their contemporary homeland. The project links different Armenian schools across the world, each with varying degrees of access to technology and training, but all wishing to strengthen their awareness of a shared personal heritage, including the Armenian language and alphabet.

The ICT curriculum for Armenian teachers is project-based and structured around a task, such as the production of a web-based newsletter. The project provides valuable strategies for the planning of curriculum across cultures and schools, which are summarised as follows:

- *Language*: Instructions and other input from the project designers are bilingual. Students work in the target language, Armenian in this case. Software has been developed to include the target language alphabet.
- *Points of contact*: Schools serving Armenian children are linked electronically to schools in Armenia in the collaborative projects. Home and community centres need careful development to act as coordinating centres for curriculum projects.
- *Informal catalyst*: An informal catalyst to collaboration is necessary. In this project, the school in Armenia always takes this role.
- *Community building*: the projects, exercise and games are specially designed for the Diaspora, including activities that introduce students new to their culture.
- *Connectivity*: The project uses a flexible set of connectivity solutions including: direct access, connectivity centres, the Web, and CD's as a means of providing wider access.

They further give guidance in setting up such a network, emphasising the important role of ICT teacher educators and leaders. There is a significant need for highly committed project managers to shepherd the project through its various stages. These stages include web and learning-activity design, identifying participants from a worldwide audience, and overcoming many logistical issues associated with adding content to a school curriculum and identifying Internet resources.

Projects such as this will be exhibited and supported through the Universal Forum of Cultures Education project. Applications to participate are available online. Guidance on the creation and support of virtual learning communities and information on potential partners may also be found in these and other web sites.

### *Quality Assurance*

Quality assurance in teacher education is an ongoing process and is demonstrated in a number of different ways. The teacher education institution itself may be scrutinised along with individual programmes within the institution. The quality of the teacher education institution and its programmes is often judged by the performance of the teachers they produce and the success of their graduates in effecting improved student learning in their P-12 classrooms. Quality assurance is often determined through an accreditation process. Demonstrated competence of teacher candidates in use of ICTs in teacher education has become increasingly important in making accreditation, certification, and programme review decisions. This is particularly true in the two countries that have adopted detailed national standards, the United States and the United Kingdom.

### *National Accreditation Standards*

In the USA, the National Council for Accreditation of Teacher Education (NCATE) recognises high quality university programmes through an accreditation process. NCATE provides national accreditation standards for the teacher education unit and for a variety of programmes within the unit, including those preparing candidates specialising in ICTs. NCATE has developed a strong collaboration with the professional association, International Society for Technology in Education (ISTE), and its standards. ISTE is responsible for recommending to NCATE the standards for pro-grammes preparing Secondary Teachers of Computer Science, school-level Technology Facilitators, and Technology Directors for districts or regional areas. ISTE is also responsible for reviewing the NCATE Programme Reports from universities seeking national recognition for their ICT programmes.

The ISTE affiliation with NCATE has resulted in strong accreditation guidelines for technology in teacher preparation programmes, as well as programmes preparing individuals for leadership roles in planning and implementing ICTs in educational environments. Guidelines are also in place identifying the requirements for technology integration throughout teacher preparation programmes, as required by the new performance-based NCATE Standards adopted in May 2000.

In their institutional report, each unit, or college of education, seeking initial accreditation is required to submit its conceptual framework outlining the philosophical and pedagogical underpinnings of the programme as a precondition for NCATE accreditation eligibility. The framework provides direction for programmes, courses, teaching, candidate performance, scholarship, service, and unit accountability. In addition to addressing the standards, the unit's document must include an overview of their institutional conceptual framework. One of six major indicators required when describing the conceptual framework is the unit's "Commitment to Technology" for the teacher preparation programme. The indicator states:

The unit's conceptual framework(s) reflects the unit's commitment to preparing candidates who are able to use educational technology to help all students learn; it also provides a conceptual understanding of how knowledge, skills, and dispositions related to educational and information technology are integrated throughout the curriculum, instruction, field experiences, clinical practice, assessments, and evaluations.

Other indicators include shared vision, coherence, professional commitments and dispositions, commitment to diversity, and candidate proficiencies aligned with professional and state standards. All universities seeking accreditation must verify their commitment to technology within their conceptual framework. Many universities reference the ISTE NETS for Teachers when preparing their descriptions of their technology commitment. In addition to clearly identifying the unit's commitment to technology in the conceptual framework, technology requirements are included within the NCATE unit standards themselves. In addition to the commitment to technology expressed in the conceptual framework for the university, the accreditation standards have also interwoven the ICT requirements throughout the assessment rubric.

### *Recommendations*

The following recommendations may help agencies and organisations in UNESCO Member States to plan curricula:

- When planning curriculum, be sure it is congruent with the educational vision, the culture, and the context of each region, both locally and globally. Develop the vision and standards in stages, starting with a core that can be expanded into a set of standards, implemented with ICTs, for the preparation and continuing professional development of teachers.

and continuing professional development of teachers.

- The ICT curriculum should facilitate change toward a more inclusive approach that promotes positive and supportive interdependence between students and teachers, while maintaining individual accountability and autonomy.
- Plan the curriculum to promote inter-cultural collaboration, and develop a learning community within and between schools and countries, using shared and complementary approaches with languages and cultures.

## Components of ICTs in Teacher Development

When a university, teacher education unit, state, region or country adopts or adapts a set of standards for determining how technology will be infused throughout their programmes, it is critical that faculty in the teacher education programmes be included in the planning effort. The faculty will plan for ICTs in teacher development considering their own conditions, culture, and context. During this collaborative planning phase, the teacher education unit and other university units providing courses for pre-service teachers (i.e. teacher candidates) should develop plans that not only address the four key components within the framework, but also the elements that support long-term implementation of the key components-leadership and vision, context and culture, planning and management of change, and lifelong learning.

These elements are necessary for a supportive environment and a successful, self-sustaining implementation of technology infusion within the teacher education programme. Experience has shown that a number of essential conditions must be met to successfully integrate ICTs into teacher education programmes. As educational entities have implemented ICTs in teacher education, researchers and evaluators have identified barriers that prevent or restrict successful technology infusion.

Teacher educators express frustration by stating, "I am having problems implementing our plan for infusion of ICTs because..." Such statements are often completed by one or more conditions quite common among teacher education institutions around the world. ISTE has compiled a list of the most commonly cited conditions necessary to create learning environments conducive to powerful uses of technology.

When planning for implementation of ICTs in teacher education, the planning team should consider each essential condition and note whether, and to what extent, it is present. The context, culture, and extent of collaboration among stakeholders will affect how adequately the conditions are met and determine what types of strategies might solicit support if the essential conditions are not currently present.

### Shared Vision

Defined as the presence of proactive leadership and administrative support, shared vision means that the commitment to technology is systemic. From the administration to the grounds personnel, there is an understanding of, commitment to, and sense of advocacy for the implementation of technology. When the implementation of a technology initiative is problematic, a major reason often cited is a breakdown in the common understanding of the institution's goals among those who hold the decision-making power. These situations can occur over something as simple as unlocking the door to a lab, or as complex as modifying existing operational budgets to provide allocations for technology funding. Facilitating the integration of technology may require a change in policy or rules, and the decision-makers have to be willing to look at the situation, forge compromises when necessary, and ensure communication among all parties. The collaborative environment necessary for creating a shared vision is also needed to sustain that vision.

### *Access to Technology*

The fact that educators need access to current technologies, software, and telecommunications networks seems simple. However, this access must be consistent across all the environments that are part of the preparation of teachers. Most teacher education programmes involve several entities, including at least a college or university and one or more schools in the P-12 range. The access to funding and other resources may vary greatly among these partners, yet ideally, access should be adequate and consistent throughout the educational experience of students in the process of becoming teachers. Creative partnerships are often required to make this happen.

Additionally, there needs to be access to technology appropriate to the subject areas being studied, such as word processing programs and Internet access in English, or computer labs and microscopes for science labs. Access must be in classrooms as well as lab settings, and provisions must be made for special populations. The technology should be accessible immediately when it is the best route to the information or tools needed by pre-service teachers, teachers, and students. Furthermore, university model classrooms are important for determining the way technology should be used in the P-12 environment. There should be an instructor station with a presentation system and 4-6 stations for pre-service teachers. The teacher candidates need to see and experience models that demonstrate the kind of access desired in the classroom. In addition to ICT access in their coursework, pre-service teachers must have technology access in their student teaching environments and in their classrooms in the induction year and beyond. Otherwise, opportunities to use technology tools for teaching students or communication tools for mentoring or staying connected with parents will be limited.

### Use of Technology

The educators who work with teacher candidates must be skilled in the use of technology for learning. They must be able to apply technology in the presentation and administration of their coursework and facilitate the appropriate use of technology by their teacher candidates. From the first course taken by a freshman, through collaborative work at the school site, pre-service teachers should participate with and observe their mentors using technology effectively. The teacher educator should model and teach techniques for managing technology in the classroom and for communicating outside the classroom through electronic means.

### Professional Development

Even in contexts in which professional development is extensive, it is important to provide consistent access to professional development as the technology constantly changes. Ongoing opportunities for professional development should be available to university and P-12 faculty and administrators who participate in the preparation of teachers. The venues and delivery mechanisms should take into consideration issues of time, location, distance, credit options, and so on. Professional development is not a one-time event it should be focused on the needs of the faculty member, teacher, or administrator and sustained through coaching and periodic updates.

### Need of Technical Assistance

Educators need technical assistance to use and maintain technology. The focus of the faculty member, teacher, and pre-service teacher should be on teaching and learning, not on maintaining and repairing the technology beyond basic troubleshooting procedures. When the technology does not function well, a learning opportunity is lost and faculty frustration grows. Timely technical assistance is imperative for faculty and candidates to feel confident that they can use technology in their teaching and learning. There are many ways technical assistance can be obtained, including asking community members or student assistants to maintain a help desk. It is a critical factor for success in implementing ICTs.

### Content Standards and Curriculum Resources

Educators must be knowledgeable in the content, standards, and teaching methodologies of their disciplines. Teacher candidates must learn to use tech-nology in powerful, meaningful ways in the context of teaching content. Technology brings relevant resources from the real world to subject area content, provides tools for analysing and synthesising data, and conveys content through a variety of media and formats. Pre-service teachers should learn to use technology in ways that meet the content standards and the technology standards for students and teachers.

### *Student-Centred Teaching*

Teaching in all settings should encompass student-centred approaches to learning. Technology should not be used only as a tool for demonstration, as an electronic overhead projector or blackboard; rather the use of technology by students should be an integral part of instruction. In student-centred approaches to learning, students become the source for problems investigated. Students and teacher candidates must have opportunities to identify problems, collect and analyse data, draw conclusions, and convey results using electronic tools to accomplish these tasks. Faculty should model the use of ICTs to demonstrate their usefulness and appropriateness for collaboration, acquisition of resources, analysis and synthesis, presentation, and publication.

### *Assessment*

In addition to assessing teaching and student outcomes, institutions should continuously assess the effectiveness of technology for learning throughout the entire teacher preparation environment. The data obtained from this continuous assessment will:

- inform the learning strategies used,
- ensure that the vision for technology-use maintains the appropriate direction,
- pinpoint potential problems,and
- provide data for altering policies and instructional strategies or for acquiring resources.

Changes made over time due to technology innovation will exemplify informed decision-making.

### Community Support

The visioning process includes the community and school partners who provide expertise, support, and resources for technology implementation. The community must see that technology is a valuable tool for prospective teachers and their students, and must be willing to support it in the political process from the boardroom to the state house.

### Support Policies

Policies can either support or hinder the implementation of technology. As decision-makers develop new policies, they must consider how the policies affect acquisition of and access to technology. Some major barriers to the use of technology relate to faculty expectations about incentives and reward structures. The expectation for the use of technology must cut across all subject areas and teacher preparation contexts so that faculty and teacher candidates are assured that their work will be valued.

Policies related to technical assistance should also support the use of technology rather than obstruct it. For example, although firewalls are essential in the university environment, there are ways to provide dial-up and remote access while maintaining the security of campus servers. Likewise, at the school level, there are ways to control students' Internet access to unwanted images and information while maintaining an environment of exploration and inquiry. Teachers and teacher educators cannot be expected to implement what they have learned about effective use of ICTs without the presence of essential conditions in their work environment. The following environments correspond to stages of development commonly experienced during university preparation:

- General Preparation-general university courses providing instruction in the foundational courses for all students and the specific coursework in the student's major field of study
- Professional Preparation-formal coursework in professional education
- Student Teaching/Internship-supervised, extended field experience in the P-12 classroom
- First-Year Teaching-the initial year of P-12 classroom teaching

Recognition of the essential conditions necessary in all the environments that contribute to the preparation of teachers underscores the shared responsibility for preparing new teachers. The university, teacher education unit, and P-12 education must advocate resources that fulfil the essential conditions for each crucial stage of teacher development.

In planning the integration of ICTs into teacher education, it is important for teacher education institutions to understand the knowledge and skills necessary for teachers to effectively use ICTs in their instruction. They must also understand the institution's level of readiness to integrate technology into the teacher education curriculum. To accomplish these goals requires that the teacher education institution understand the benchmarks, standards, and guidelines for ICTs in teacher education. It is also important that they have access to tools that help them assess their level of readiness and progress in infusing ICTs into the teacher education programmes.

# 4

# Web-based Teaching Methods

Communication media establish forms of interaction and kinds of social and political relations by virtue of the structural conditions that they impose. In broad outline, medium theorists point to 3 or 4 phases of civilisation with corresponding forms of communication, from oral societies, to print societies (via a scribal phase), to an electronic (global) culture. The differences between these types of communication are certain structural conditions that each type of medium imposes and consequently in built effects to which they give rise. Thus in oral societies communicative interaction requires participants to share the same space and time, employing a multiplicity of symbolic cues. By contrast, in print societies, participants may be located in contexts that are spatially and temporally distinct and the symbolic cues available to participants are narrowed and standardised.

Moreover, and like electronic media, print is not necessarily oriented towards specific others. Rather, symbolic forms may address an indefinite potential audience. The implications for the teaching and learning environments may not be immediately obvious but they are highly significant. Since the activity of teaching requires effective communication we need tc ask what are the structural effects that CMC via the Internet, and the WWW impose which differentiates them from traditional print and oral teaching methods. In what ways does the use of CMC, change the teaching and learning environment?

Without understanding the structural conditions imposed by different types of communication media, we cannot appreciate the change brought about by the new technologies or their potential. Structural conditions and effects of different communication media in the teaching and learning environment. The traditional method of teaching arts and social science courses and particularly political science relies on a combination of lectures, tutorials, seminars, exams and individual student research - mostly in the form of essay writing which involves reading and analysing books and articles pertinent to the researched subject.

Lectures are mostly structured as a uni-directional form of face to face communication, addressing the students *en masse.* The lecturer usually stands or walks around the lecture theatre in front of the students while the students are all seated (hopefully) in silence, listening and busily taking notes. Lecturers sometimes also avail themselves to the blackboard to provide in written form the names of significant authors, titles of significant works, lecture outlines, important concepts and other information. Though lecturers may quote from different sources they are the authors of the lecture. By contrast, seminars and tutorials in which discussion takes place, are bi-directional forms of communication.

Students and tutors take turns in addressing each other and the class, in a multi-participant conversation. Thus the structure of these environments allows for joint authorship of these 'events'. But again, like in lectures, speakers and audience must take turns in authoring utterances. All three are 'events' that take place at a specific time and at a specific location on campus requiring the attendance of all parties. In other words they are synchronous communication 'events' requiring the presence of participants. Moreover, lecture theatres, seminar and tutorial rooms place limits to the number of students that can attend any particular 'event'.

The structure of these communicative 'events' places a high premium on the knowledge of the lecturers and tutors placing them at the centre of the knowledge acquisition and distribution process. Knowledge is selected and passed on from the lecturers to the students and is corrected, reinforced, added to, explained, and evaluated for the students by the lecturers and tutors who are accepted as authoritative. Individual student research in the form of essays and papers on the other hand, does not require the student to be present in any particular time or place for the learning process to occur.

It does however require them to attend to printed communication media - books, article etc., - that unlike the 'event' character of the lectures and tutorials are 'objects' with definite size and spatial characteristics. Thus, as materials in the teaching environment they too are restricted by availability to the space occupied by the student and time it takes to access them. While listening to lectures and participating in discussions in seminars and tutorials does not require any particular skills - though at the university level it does require a certain level of oral competence and knowledge - reading texts and writing does require specific learned skills. These skills are learned prior to their participation at university courses and are supposedly enhanced and expanded through the practice of essay and paper writing.

The form of communication involved in these practices is asynchronous, with authorship being highly significant and strictly defined. Books have definite authors who are located in different time and space to the students and are thus, unlike lecturers and tutors, unavailable to explain or be questioned about their message. Which and how many authors and works a student uses in research and writing usually has important implications for assessing the quality of the essay and knowledge of the student. The importance of authorship is specifically reinforced by strict penalties surrounding the issue of plagiarism.

Printed books and articles used in the traditional teaching environment, are also characterised by their linear and sequential presentation of material. This it has been argued, contributes to rational and logical thinking. Students are expected to emulate this form in their own authoring endeavours. The essay or paper authored by the student is an individual response to the 'objects' and 'events' in the course. It itself becomes an 'object' that is taken to represent the knowledge gained by the student from the 'objects' and 'events' presented in the course. And indeed they usually form a significant part of the assessment of the students achievement in the course.

Written exams on the other hand, like lectures, tutorials and seminars, are usually 'events' that occur at definite times and locations. They require student presence. However, the product of exams, the written paper, like the essay, is an 'object' used to assess student knowledge. There is however a number of types of exams including oral exams or take-home exams. The former requires presence by the student and is a synchronous communicative 'event' while the latter does not require student presence and is thus an asynchronous 'event' producing an essay type 'object'.

In short, the structural conditions imposed by traditional communication media in the teaching and learning environment include oral uni-directional and bi-directional communication forms whose effect is to privilege authorship and authority of lecturers and tutors in the acquisition and distribution of knowledge; they involve both synchronous and asynchronous forms of communication that, apart from student research essays, require participants to be present in specific locations and at specific times; and they give priority to the printed written form, privileging linear sequential and rational modes of individual thinking made into 'objects' for assessing student knowledge.

## Internet and WWW

CMC made its first appearance for pedagogical practice in the arts and social science in the late 1970's and early 1980's mostly as tools for word processing and statistical analysis. By the early 1990's the Internet and the WWW began to make inroads into the arts and social science courses as tools for communication and resources. Perhaps the most radical feature of the new communication media is the alterations it makes to the structural conditions of oral, written, and graphical means of communication. It integrates many of the technologies of communication and information processing developed in the last century into a virtual space shattering many of the structural conditions imposed by the other means of communication.

In contrast to traditional lectures, tutorials, seminars, exams etc., CMC via the Internet and the WWW enables both synchronous and asynchronous communication. It means that both uni-directional and bi-directional, as well as multi-directional communication can take place. And it means that both 'events' and 'objects' can be presented simultaneously- though it changes the limitations of both. In short it means that all our pedagogical means of communication can be used simultaneously whilst many of their limitations transcended.

Consider the structural condition of the traditional lecture or seminar as a synchronous communication 'event' that requires presence in a certain time and location, and consequently the limit on student numbers in a lecture theatre or seminar room. Using CMC via the WWW such a lecture can remain a synchronous communication 'event', yet not require presence of participants at the same location. And it also enables an indefinite number of students to attend. Moreover that same 'event' can be reproduced on demand as an asynchronous 'event' ie it can become a virtual 'event' that a student can download or trigger online at a different time. The effect is that students rather than lecturers and tutors are placed at the centre of the knowledge acquisition process.

The use of CMC via the Internet and WWW to communicate both student authored essays and 'authorised' texts (usually called: recommended Readings) - the 'objects' - creates even a more radical transformation to the structural conditions imposed by written and printed communication media. It adds a dimension of interconnectivity of texts as hypertexts and it transforms the 'objective' fixity of the text. Moreover collaborative and joint authorship enabled in seminars and tutorials become optional extras in textual form to a multitude of students simultaneously - copies of text can be reproduced and transferred electronically on demand. It also changes the very process of linear reading as readers must move back and forth from linear presentation of the written, the iconic and graphical.

The problem of textual non-linearity and non-sequential reading, which in Stephanie Gibson's apt phrase 'crack open the relationship between user and text', has been raised by a number of writers. The concern is that a cognitive 'bottleneck' or overload may be the result of the multi-modal processing inherent in multimedia presentation systems. In other words the concern is that the mental resources required for coding and decoding will result in decrease in comprehension. Attention paid to graphic and iconic elements might detracts from narrative and from coherent logical and rational thought.

As Susan Barnes points out, it may be creating a new type of post-literate style of communication that substitutes emotional forms of visual persuasion for the strength of logic. Today the core skills, apart from reading and writing, include basic computer familiarity, word processing, telecommunications knowledge including dial-in procedures, online tools including FTP, Telnet, E-mail and web browser familiarity, online library searches, download routines and ability to use system software for all these functions. In short, the structural conditions imposed by CMC via the Internet and WWW make traditional pedagogical practices more malleable to variations of delivery.

Lectures and tutorials that necessitated synchronous presence can now be delivered in both synchronous and asynchronous communication forms. The effect is to make students the centre of the knowledge acquisition process, allowing them to select and attend classes in accordance with their needs and availability - class timetable clashes can become a thing of the past. Use of the new communication media also transform the way students, and teachers for that matter, research, read and write. Using hypertext, textual linearity and sequential reading and writing give way to interconnection and collaborative writing. While the problem of necessary additional skills needed to use the new technology is significant, the experience of the Simulation at Melbourne, shows it is solvable - moreover far from distracting attention from narrative and logical thought, as we shall see, it can enhance contextual thinking.

## Simulations of Real-time Environments

In one way or another, simulations of real-time environments have been used as a tool for teaching in many areas and disciplines. This has been the case especially in areas like medicine or in the art of war, where pedagogical practice in real-time environments carries too high a risk. It is also used where access to real-time environments is either restricted or very limited as in law, which is restricted to certified professionals or as in space exploration, which is too costly. Moreover, in multivariate environments where outcomes from initial conditions are difficult, if not impossible, to predict with any measure of accuracy, it is often useful to use simulations to evaluate possible outcomes.

The idea behind using simulations as pedagogical tools relies on the idea that experience is the best teacher. If access to such experience in real-time is for some reason not possible, than for teaching purposes an artificially created environment may be, if not ideal, at least sufficient. Combined with the fact that the structural conditions of traditional pedagogical communication media have been transformed by the new technologies, it seems reasonable to think that the new multimedia potential of CMC which enable us to create artificial environments for pedagogical purposes, would be used for that purpose more extensively.

There are at least 3 types of simulations currently used for teaching. The first, and more traditional type of simulation involves CMC only incidentally. This type relies on a conference like setting in which all participants are available to each other in the same location e.g. UN Model simulation. The second type of simulation is the computer generated simulation. This types which appears as a software program, more often on CD-ROM, is really designed for single users, who feed variables into the program which then uses them to construct an environment appropriate to these variables in the particular field that the program aims to simulate e.g. CASCON developed at MIT and Exploring the Nardoo River System and Stagestruck developed at the University of Wollongong.

The third type, and the one which we will report on here, is the Web-based simulation in which CMC is used to create a space in which students playing roles connect to each other and generate the simulation activity in the field being learned. Although a number of Web-based simulations have appeared in different disciplines, including Nursing, organizational writing, and other courses, the uptake for such simulations has been slow. It seems that redesigning courses away from the traditional pedagogical model is not as popular as it could be.

One explanation for this is that lecturers used to traditional pedagogical practices are reluctant to engage with the new technology for various reasons, including lack of familiarity with the technology, lack of institutional commitment and support, lack of equipment etc. While these reasons may indeed explain reluctance, there are at least 2 strong arguments which suggest that the instructional value of using CMC and simulations should persuade them to make that extra effort to overcome the obstacles.

The first argument is that inherent to the design of simulations is that it is a problem-solving activity within a context. Current thinking on learning and instructional design emphasises precisely the utility of learning activity within context. Viewing learning from this perspective means two things. Firstly it means that the social, interpersonal and cultural surroundings within which learning occurs affect both the learning process and outcomes. Secondly, 'within context' also means that the skills, strategies, and learning processes are seen as being tightly connected to their immediate contexts of practice rather than as neutral tools available for varied general application. In other words, they are seen as highly situated.

The second argument is that the structural conditions of CMC, as we have pointed out earlier, provide great flexibility in synchronous and asynchronous communication and joint authorship of 'events' (like seminars & tutorials). This capacity is thus tailor-made for what in educational literature is known as collaborative learning.

As described by one researcher, collaboration is "the mutual engagement of participants in a coordinated effort to solve a problem together." Some of the critical features of this concept are that it is based on doing something; that the engagement of learners is cooperative as opposed to competitive behaviour; and there is a shift in the instructors role from provider of information to facilitator of the learning process.

## Simulations in Political Science

The use of CMC simulations as a teaching tool in Political Science began in the early 1990s with the collaborative pioneering work of Dr. Andrew Vincent in the Political Science Department and Dr. John Sheppard in the Computer Science Department, both at Melbourne University. Their first models were really E-mail based simulations but since 1994 Web pages were added to enhance the simulation with pages for role profiles, research resources and other pages.

In 1998 Dr. Peter Shearman and Mr. Roni Linser received a $5000 Project grant from Melbourne university to develop a pilot simulation for the World Politics in Transition course run by Dr. Shearman at the Political Science Department. The pilot simulation was designed to supplement a lecture-based course focusing on theories with a hands-on approach to World Politics. The course which aimed to familiarise students with different approaches and theories to World Politics, until 1997, relied on the traditional approach of lectures, tutorials and individual research by students. Students were assessed on the bases of a 3000 word essay and a 2-hour exam at the end of the course. The new course, run in the second semester of 1998, used a Web site, designed by Mr. Roni Linser (aided by the technical officer of the Political Science Dept, Mr. David Lutz), whose pages were an interactive space for students to examine the political processes and theories introduced in the lectures.

The simulation began with a Scenario to which the different roles reacted. The Scenario, written up by the lecturers in-charge, was set up in accordance with real world events adding fictional events. It was set around the possibility of the acquisition of nuclear weapons by Iran hoping to stimulate the various actors in the simulation to ponder upon the repercussions of such a possibility and to provide likely responses from the perspective of their role. The simulation ended with a face to face conference, like a UN General Assembly Meeting, at which each team presented position papers of their role and negotiated agreements to resolve (where possible) any outstanding issues arising during the simulation.

The most significant design aspects of the simulation were the allocation of each role to a team rather than to individual students, the development of a scenario that demanded response from every role; and an environment for learning that moved between the Web site, the E-mail system and face to face interaction with peers, lecturer and tutors. The logic of playing in small teams was based on experience from previous simulations. The amount of work required to keep up with events in the simulation was large - it included initiating events, reading incoming E-mail, evaluating possible responses, researching information and responding. On average it required about 1 to 2 hours per day over the three week period (including weekends).

Playing in teams rather than individuals, allowed the students to organize their time and responsibilities amongst themselves so that they were not overloaded with work. It also, and significantly, provided them with a partner or partners with whom they could discuss and analyse various options. The importance of the scenario as the initial condition of the simulation, is that it functioned as a set of themes to consider, and contexts for activity through out the simulation. This was the problem, or rather set of problems, designed by the lecturer and tutors, that each team needed to address. Their initial responses in turn created new problems that needed resolution and so forth. Thus from the initial context provided by the scenario, new contexts were generated by the activity of students, to which they needed to respond. This continuous shifting context was the reason why so much work was required.

Understanding politics, and in particular International relations, requires precisely this understanding of shifting contexts. Theories of International relations attempt to explain and perhaps predict the behaviour of the international system But to understand the degree to which they are able to do so requires students to understand the fact that this system is in continuous flux. In the simulation, it was precisely their own actions which demonstrated to them this flux. The contexts provided by the fictional scenario to which students responded was framed by a number of other contexts - by the real-world political context, by the educational context of the course, by the context of the students social networks and by the context of the role which they were playing.

The environment created by the simulation thus put students in a number of contexts simultaneously. The Web site provided them with links to real-world events and actors; the lectures and tutorials continuously linked them to the course, the lecturer and tutors and to their peers; and this was reinforced by collaborative work in the simulation; while the E-mail system functioned as a linkage between the different roles being played. What the simulation achieved was a process of teaching and learning politics in a number of contexts through collaboration.

While collaborative learning, as we pointed out earlier requires the engagement of learners in a cooperative as opposed to competitive behaviour, learning about politics without understanding competitive behaviour is like trying to learn to swim without water. In short, the simulation enabled students to learn through the experience of both cooperation and competition simultaneously. In the context of their team they worked through cooperation, while within the context of other roles, they sought to work both in cooperation or in competition depending on the goals of their role and the contexts which they themselves created.

## Resources for Teaching

The internet is bursting with political science teaching and learning resources. A Google search for 'political science resources' returns over 1.8 million sites. And the number grows daily. Many sites are of very high quality. Some of the best are government sites. The United States government portal is the most impressive. It provides a comprehensive gateway through which citizens, employees and businesses can interact with the federal government and its agencies. Teachers and students can use the portal to access government data, and many government agencies have made great efforts to ensure that access to data is as simple and straightforward as possible.

Indeed, the range and quality of the data available is staggering. Interested parties can use the FedWorld Information Network or FedStats to access government information and databases. The US Census Bureau maintains a particularly comprehensive and impressive website. Users can search for aggregate pre-packaged census results, and use interactive internet tools to retrieve and analyse individual-level data on-line. Alternatively, users can download census data direct to their PCs. However, in spite of concerted government efforts to facilitate easy access to and use of such data, its intrinsic complexity and size makes it problematic.

While other governments, especially in western democracies, have begun to follow America's lead in using the internet to (re-)connect with their citizens, their efforts hitherto are neither as comprehensive nor sophisticated. However, the smaller size of non-American government sites makes them more navigable and intuitively attractive, especially for novice users. The United Kingdom's new portal, UK Online, is a good example. It facilitates access to over 1,000 government and public service websites, including the National Statistics Online, which publishes summaries of national statistics and allows users to download individual-level data. However, as is the case with the US Census pages, there are few on-line teaching and learning resources. Other government websites suffer similar problems.

Most universities in the US and UK have a dedicated 'political science resource site', usually hosted and managed by either the university library or the political science department. In the main, these sites contain little other than a long list of links to other government and politics websites: for example, to the White House, Congress, the Supreme Court, state governments, pressure groups and so on. The resource sites usually also include links to a multitude of data sources, such as the US Census Bureau, ICPSR, Eurostat and the UK Data Archive. Increasingly, academics are providing on-line access to specially constructed datasets on their own webpages, and many university resource pages provide the necessary links.

A number of 'gateway' sites perform a similar function. For example, the Social Science Information Gateway provides a long list of political resources, but does not differ in any substantive way from most university sites. It is our sense that most resource sites do not provide a particularly efficacious service. Many are ill organised, and users can spend too long searching recommended sites without finding the appropriate information or data. Most resource sites hosted by professional associations such as the American Political Science Association and the (British) Political Studies Association offer a similar type and level of service.

Google or other such proprietary search engines offer a more simple and efficient way to locate one's object, so long as users know what data they want and were it is hosted. For inexperienced users, however, university and educational association sites are a good first port of call, as they introduce users to a wide range of sites and data that they may not otherwise have thought existed. In addition to problems of structure and organisation, most university and educational association resource sites suffer one major problem: replication. The resource links are almost identical across sites. While replication is not a major concern for the end user, it represents an extremely inefficient use of funds and time. Thousands (or perhaps tens of thousands) of people are writing and managing almost identical sites. Centralisation could in this case result in significant savings.

Another problem is that few university and educational association websites provide access to easily usable data resources. There are, however, some exceptions. For example, the University of Michigan hosts the National Election Studies homepage. Here, users can download NES individual-level data and codebooks. Users can also access the NES Guide to Public Opinion and Electoral Behavior, which contains time-series trends across a range of issues. This is a fast, efficient, well-organised and maintained site that delivers an impressive amount of information in a user-friendly way. However, users are not able to construct their own tables and graphs from NES individual-level data. Nor are they able to cross-tabulate different variables.

Nevertheless, it an excellent site. While the British Election Study does not yet offer users an NES-style time-series facility, NESSTAR allows users to run basic statistical tests on cross-sectional data on-line and to download subsets of individual-level data to analyse on their own PC. As the number of datasets available via NESSTAR increases, so will its utility to the academic community. However, it is as yet unclear whether NESSTAR is user-friendly enough to attract inexperienced data and student users.

## Web-based Learning and Teaching Sites

More recently, funding bodies and organisations have begun to think creatively and constructively about ways in which the internet can be used in training and learning. JISC has already funded a wide range of projects designed to "integrate learning environments with the wider information landscape aimed at increasing the use of online electronic resources" through its 5/99 Learning and Teaching Programme. One example is the Resource Discovery Network's recently published Virtual Training Suite, a series of free web-based tutorials designed to "develop...internet research and information skills." The site allows users to choose from a wide range of tutorials. Each tutorial directs users (whether teachers, students or researchers) to the most relevant and important websites (e.g. government portals, library catalogues, journals, databases etc.).

While the tutorials are very well designed and include a host of special features not seen elsewhere (for example, a links basket to collect links to key sites, and quizzes to test users' knowledge), the links are often no different to those found on most university resource pages. Moreover, the aim of each tutorial is to improve people's internet skills, not their grasp of substantive issues. Biz/ed, another website funded by RDN in partnership with MIMAS, pushes the boundaries of internet learning. Aimed at teachers and students of economics, business and accounting, it allows users to use real data to learn about substantive and statistical issues. The main interface through which users access data is TimeWeb-"a unique integrated package of data and teaching and learning materials to support the teaching of data skills." It is a model of its kind, and free to Biz/ed users.

TimeWeb is itself a JISC-funded project; the central aim is to re-purpose macro-economic time-series datasets as key learning and teaching resources. Although economic, not political science, data are the intended object, it may be possible to use TimeWeb in our own project. Even if this is not the case, we can learn much from the layout and pedagogic approach of Biz/ed-TimeWeb. Another good 5/99 example is the CHCC project, which aims to integrate census data into learning and teaching programmes in HE by "improving accessibility to the primary data resources; developing an integrated set of learning and teaching materials; improving awareness about the contexts in which Census data can be used in learning and teaching; integrating contextual materials; providing access to web-based data exploration/visualisation tools; [and] developing resource discovery tools via a Census portal."

The teaching and learning materials include eight units focusing on various aspects of nineteenth century Britain. Each uses census data to improve users' understanding of urbanisation, migration, household and family structure and so on. The site also contains materials to support the analysis of contemporary samples of anonymised records (SARs), including teaching units on data analysis and substantive issues such as social class, ethnicity, inequality and education. As with the Biz/ed site discussed above, the CHCC project should prove an invaluable guide for writing and piloting our own political science site. Another very good site that aims to bring real data into the classroom is the JISC-funded Stars project, a joint effort of De Montford, Coventry, Kingston, Nottingham Trent and Oxford Brookes universities.

Stars, creating statistical resources from real datasets, "aims to make available real datasets, from accessible databases, in a form suitable for a learning and teaching resource in HE across a range of disciplines, construct learning materials to accompany these datasets, and develop materials so they can be used with various statistical packages for a range of student abilities, backgrounds and needs." Users, primarily undergraduates, download data to their PCs in an Excel file, and then use one of five statistical packages (hosted locally) to analyse the data. While our own project focuses on political science data, Stars will, when completed, be multidisciplinary in its appeal. As yet, however, only one 'worksheet' (investigating the relationship between changes in weight loss and triglyceride level) is operational. More are planned, but the timeframe is uncertain.

# 5

# Teaching Democratic Values

Education for democracy is just as important in mature democracies, but it is often taken for granted or ignored. People grow complacent about their political system if it is working well, and they may question whether democracy even needs to be studied and learned. Some bend so far in the direction of relativism or self-criticism that they lose their zeal for and confidence in democracy. The result is that democracy gets very little attention; sometimes, it is even denounced. Although the desire for freedom may be innate, knowledge of how democracy functions must be taught and learned. Any society that wishes to remain free needs to ensure that its citizens are well educated in the theory and practice of democracy. Part of the responsibility for such education lies with the schools, which may teach children not only through the formal curriculum, but also through the conduct of their institutional affairs and through various extracurricular activities.

Yet, formal schooling is not the only educational influence in a free society. Informal sources—courses and workshops for adults, programs on television and radio, articles in newspapers and magazines, activities organized by community groups—can also help citizens of all ages learn about democracy. Anyone who doubts the political importance of education would do well to note how vigorously totalitarian and authoritarian governments work to control the information that is passed through the schools, media, and other sources. Those who have successfully struggled to overcome such regimes detest this practice of indoctrination and want to avoid it in the future.

But the absence of a totalitarian government does not magically give rise to a strong, stable, and effective democracy. Democracy does not teach itself. If the strengths, benefits, and responsibilities of democracy are not made clear to the citizens, they will be ill-equipped to defend it. Education for democracy, therefore, must be approached in a conscious and serious manner. What makes democracy education different from the indoctrination practiced by totalitarians? Primarily the habits of mind and discourse that democracy education confers, at least when properly done.

A focus on democracy does not preclude the open study of other doctrines or systems of government. Nor does it seek to hide democracy's flaws. Democracies, in contrast to other governments, are honest about their own shortcomings and truthful about those of other countries. If students are taught about the institutions, values, promises, and problems that have historically characterized democracy, and those that have characterized alternate forms of government, there is little doubt that they will come to appreciate and cherish the democratic political system. They will not necessarily regard it as perfect. It seldom is. But they will realize that it is the best system of government yet tried—and perhaps the most difficult to maintain.

Children in emerging democracies, having previously attended schools dedicated to ensuring that democratic ideas did not take root, can be expected to understand and prize democracy only if their education system is rapidly and thoroughly transformed. Yet where teachers and principals have not themselves lived in democracy, nor even been allowed to study it, and where textbooks and other instructional materials have been designed to suppress and undermine democratic ideas, such a transformation is an immense undertaking. Much work thus lies ahead for those tending to the education systems of aspiring democracies. Fortunately, they need not start from scratch. Democracy education has been practiced successfully in many lands, including a number of the newer democracies.

Any effort at democracy education must begin with a clear picture of what is to be taught and learned. It is, therefore, crucial that those designing education programs, and those who will be teaching in them, possess an informed understanding of democracy. Unfortunately, despite its current vogue, "democracy" is a term that is often misunderstood and misused. Totalitarian and military regimes, for example, may call themselves democratic republics and showcase constitutions promising rights and freedoms that are, in reality, nonexistent. Furthermore, in countries emerging from totalitarianism, where oppression has been the norm for decades, there may be a tendency to view democracy simplistically, as a guarantee of individual freedom, even license, rather than as a complex interplay of ideas, institutions, obligations, rights, and actions.

Democracy is a system of self-government where the citizens are equal and political decisions are made by majority rule, but always with the protection of minority rights. In its purest form, democracy affords citizens the opportunity to participate directly in the decision-making process. This is called direct democracy. But given the size and complexity of today's societies, it is generally more practical for citizens to elect representatives who will govern and make decisions on their behalf. Representative democracy relies on regular, free, fair, and competitive elections to hold the government accountable to the people.

In a democracy, the government exists to serve the people, not the other way around. Since democratic government derives its authority from the consent of the governed, the people have the capacity to change the government peacefully when they lose confidence in it. And they need not fear a bullet if they try. While majority rule is the bedrock principle upon which democracy rests, simple majoritarianism has its own drawbacks. Hence it usually operates within a constitutional framework that limits the power of government and safeguards individual and minority rights. In such constitutional democracies, all citizens possess certain fundamental rights, and the exercise of those rights by minorities does not depend upon the goodwill of the majority.

Such rights are guaranteed through mechanisms that are extremely difficult to alter. In the United States, for example, the Constitution lists freedom of speech, freedom of religion, freedom of assembly, and the right to a fair trial as inalienable rights of all citizens. The state and national governments are forbidden from passing any law that denies or erodes these rights. Also fundamental to democratic government are the checks and balances that block any institution, group, or individual from becoming too powerful. It is important, for example, to have an independent judiciary that can prevent the executive and legislative branches from overstepping their bounds.

In the United States, the executive and the Congress operate separately to provide further checks on each other.

In this way, no one person or even a single branch of government can amass enough power to threaten or violate citizens' rights. Although parliamentary and presidential systems differ in how they divide the powers of government, they all provide some mechanisms to limit the power of any branch. But just as democracy can fail if the government has too much power, it can also fail if government does not have enough power. The democratic process is a formula for fairness, not passivity or anarchy. Leadership is accordingly necessary for the success of democratic government, and citizens must abide by decisions of their elected leaders and obey the laws of the society.

Contrary to some perceptions, a healthy democratic society is not simply an arena where individuals pursue their private agendas. It may be the promise of freedom and opportunity that makes democracy so attractive, but just as important to its success—and all too often ignored—are the responsibilities and habits of mind that must accompany life in a democratic society. Democratic citizens are, for example, expected to participate in the political life of their society and to lend their influence to the public debate. To participate effectively, people must inform themselves about the issues affecting society and be able to weigh self-interest and factional interest against concern for the public good. They must be tolerant of dissenting views and able to cooperate and compromise. They must exhibit respect for law and legitimate authority as well as for privacy and property. Democracy is thus more than a system of government. It is a way of living and working together. And it is only when the manifold responsibilities of democratic life are taken seriously by citizens that its rights and rewards will be meaningful.

## Opportunities and Responsiblities

In order for people to understand and appreciate their opportunities and responsibilities as democratic citizens, they must receive a sound education. Such an education seeks not only to familiarize people with the precepts and practices of democracy, but also to produce citizens who are principled, independent, inquisitive, and analytic in their outlook and committed to democracy. Education for democracy should not be viewed as an isolated subject, taught for a short time each day and otherwise ignored. It is linked to nearly everything else that students learn in school—whether it be history, civics, ethics, or economics—and to much that goes on outside of school. In short, good democracy education is part of good education in general.

Education for democracy occurs in a variety of venues. The most common environment is the schools, which, in a democracy, are not controlled by government alone. Democratic governments do provide schooling for their citizens—which must be equally accessible to all, and not be used as a vehicle for government propaganda—but democracy allows for alternatives as well. Churches and other religious groups are free to create religious schools; private citizens may organize independent schools; and parents may even choose to teach their children at home. This pluralism is part of democracy; it is healthy for the society. It may also result in better education.

## School-based Democracy Education

School-based democracy education can take many forms. Within the school curriculum, the history, principles, and practice of democracy may be treated as a distinct course of study or worked into a number of other disciplines (including history, geography, economics, literature, and social studies). Alternatively, these ideas may be viewed as a theme around which an entire history/social studies curriculum can be organized. However the curriculum is structured, it must cover four fundamental areas if students are to have a sufficient understanding of and appreciation for democracy. First, adequate attention must be paid to the roots and branches of the democratic idea as well as to the history of its expansion throughout the world. Students must learn where and how the principles of democracy were born, paying close attention to the circumstances in which they emerged.

Democracy should be traced from its various strands in the classical world of the Greeks and Romans and in the ethical thought of biblical Jews and early Christians, through the Middle Ages, the Renaissance and the Reformation, the English Revolution, the Enlightenment, and the American and French revolutions. This course of study includes the examination of important historical documents such as the Magna Carta; the United States Declaration of Independence, Constitution, and Bill of Rights; and the French Declaration of the Rights of Man and the Citizen. Students should also be familiar with the history of 20th century struggle for democracy against Fascism, Communism, and other forms of dictatorship.

Second, the curriculum must help students explore how the ideas of democracy have been translated into institutions and practices around the world and through the ages. Examples of the growth and development of democratic societies of the past and present should be introduced and questions raised:

- Where has democracy flourished, where has it failed, and why?

- What political, economic, social, and cultural conditions have helped shape democratic societies?
- What conditions have hindered democratic development?
- Who has defended democracy and who has sought its undoing?
- How have democratic governments been organized to allow for majority rule? To protect individual and minority rights? To provide law and order without suppressing freedom and individualism?
- What types of non-governmental bodies have influenced the political process?
- How have legal systems been structured to limit government control and ensure that all people have the right to a fair trial?
- How have the mass media functioned?

In answering questions such as these, students will be exposed to many practical elements of a functioning democracy. They will learn how democracy works in reality—and how reality does and does not keep faith with theory. Third, the curriculum must explore the history of democracy in the students own nations, so that they may answer questions such as: What forms of government have existed in my country in the past? Have we ever tried democracy before? If so, why did it fail? What led to the establishment of our present democratic government? How are the circumstances we now face similar to those faced by democratic societies in the past? How are they different? What lessons can we learn from failed attempts at democracy in our own society and in others?

Fourth, students need to understand the current condition of democracy in the world. They must know where it exists, where it is being fought for, and what its alternatives are. They need to recognize that democracy has taken different forms in different countries, and they should understand how and why this occurs. How is Costa Rican democracy different from Australian democracy? How are they similar? What are the barriers to democracy in countries such as China, Cuba, and Iraq? What has enabled so many other nations recently to overcome these impediments? What dangers and choices lie ahead for aspiring democracies, and how can they work together—and with other, more established democratic nations—to achieve success?

Curriculum and instruction can be approached in myriad ways, but these four elements are essential for any strong democracy education program. Even in established democracies, most schools pay too little attention to the history and principles of democracy. As a result, generations of schoolchildren do not fully understand or appreciate the political system in which they live. They have come to take democracy for granted. Recently, however, some U.S. school systems have begun to adopt curriculum frameworks that offer guidelines on how better to integrate the study of democratic ideas into the educational system, and their experiences can be instructive for new democracies.

A curriculum framework is not designed for classroom use. Rather, it serves as a foundation upon which classroom materials, lesson plans, teacher guides, assessment mechanisms, and teacher training programs can be built. For example, in 1987 the State of California adopted a new curriculum framework designed to strengthen the teaching of history and social science in its elementary and secondary schools. The framework is an excellent illustration of how democratic content may be built into the formal school curriculum.

The introduction to the framework states what types of knowledge and intellectual qualities students in a democratic society—and the United States in particular—need to acquire. They must perceive the complexity of social, economic, and political problems. They should know their rights and responsibilities as citizens and understand the Constitution as a social contract that defines democratic government and guarantees individual rights. They must respect the right of others to disagree with them. They must be active citizens, and know how to work for peaceful change in society. They ought to understand the importance and the fragility of democratic institutions. They should recognize the conditions that encourage democracy to prosper and those that work against it. Finally, they should develop a keen sense of ethics and citizenship and care deeply about the quality of life in their community, their nation, and their world. In their final year of high school, students take a course that focuses specifically on the principles of American democracy.

Likewise, the Center for Civic Education, a private U.S. organization, recently published a curriculum framework for civic education in an attempt to make it a more prominent part of the curriculum in secondary schools throughout the country. Civitas, as the framework is called, features an interdisciplinary approach and focuses on the nature and politics of democratic government and the fundamental values, rights, and responsibilities of citizenship. A diverse and distinguished array of American historians, political scientists, and educators contributed to Civitas, and their hope is that it will provide the basis for some very dynamic textbooks and other curriculum materials. Recently, the Center—working with numerous

U.S. and international educators, professional organizations, civic leaders, community groups and others—has completed the National Standards for Civics and Government.

These voluntary standards for students in kindergarten through grade 12 (K-12), are intended to help schools develop competent and responsible citizens who possess a reasoned commitment to the fundamental values and principles that are essential to the preservation and improvement of American constitutional democracy. It is expected that this document will provide guidance in the development of U.S. civic education programs for years to come.

### *Methods for Teaching*

How do we teach children about democracy? This question is vibrantly alive today. Educators are more concerned than ever about teaching citizenship and democratic values. But the act of asking this question leads us to even deeper and more fundamental ones.

Does teaching democracy mean:

- Inculcating religious values, such as the Ten Commandments and other principles?
- Developing children's self-esteem, autonomous decision making, and ability to clarify values?
- Training good corporate citizens, who are neat, prompt, obedient, productive, and respectful of authority?
- Raising the consciousness of young people about the history of oppression in a capitalist, racist, and sexist society?

– None of the above, because the curriculum should be limited to academic fundamentals?

Each of these choices has its proponents—serious, well-intentioned people who believe that theirs is the right way. But all such "true believers," to use Eric Hoffer's memorable phrase, have missed the point. *There is no right way to teach democracy unless we also practice it.*

Education for democracy can be approached in a manner appropriate to students at the elementary, secondary, or post-secondary levels. Whatever the age of the student, pedagogy is naturally most effective when it captures his or her imagination. Teaching democracy lends itself well to such creativity and excitement. Students can read textbooks, monographs, biographies, autobiographies, heroic tales, poetry, and other works discussing and illuminating aspects of democracy. They may study primary documents, such as democratic charters and constitutions. They may put on plays or skits dealing with important issues or events. They may even play games, solve puzzles, and hold contests.

One useful way to inform students about their government and the democratic political system is to invite government officials, critics, and analysts to visit the classroom and answer students questions. This will not only teach children how government works, but it will also help bring it to life. Another way to make democracy vivid for students is to incorporate it into everyday classroom activities. Give students some say in matters affecting the class. Let them vote on certain issues. Allow them to work in teams, teach other children, allocate resources, make presentations, and lead class discussions. All these activities require skills vital to democratic life, skills that are often best learned through experience rather than didactically.

Teachers may encourage democratic behavior through their classroom techniques as well. Lecturing to a class is not always the best way to reach students. Students should be involved in discussions and encouraged to ask questions. If they are timid or cannot seem to come up with any questions or comments, the teacher must ask questions and stimulate discussion. This is one of the most difficult things for students in newly free societies to get used to, but it is an essential element of democracy education. Questioning is the beginning of wisdom.

### *Elementary Education*

Civic education is an important component of elementary education. Early schooling should introduce young students to the norms of American constitutional order and to the ways in which participation in American democracy has been expanded. Students in upper primary grades receive their first instruction in American history and the foundations of American democracy and in their state's history and government. Political science training will provide elementary teachers concepts and context needed to introduce these topics and relate them to the rights and responsibilities of citizenship.

Elementary school teachers are advised to take at least two semesters of political science, but four semesters is preferable. At least one semester of American Government and politics should be required, and courses in comparative government and politics and state and local government are recommended. The political science major includes courses on democratic theory, constitutional democracy, and political institutions and processes that are the core of precollege instruction on civics and government. Moreover, the subjects and skills of a political science major are compatible with a broader social sciences/social studies perspective. As a discipline, political science encompasses methods of inquiry of the cognate social science disciplines and encourages its majors to elect courses in these disciplines. For the future teacher, historical analysis is a valuable tool for political science courses and for a minor.

A pre-service teacher majoring in political science who minors in history should be qualified to teach history as well as civics and government. Political science students study government systems as well as comparative, multicultural, and international perspectives on political life. Their training emphasizes mastery of written and oral communications skills and analytical skills which precollege teachers of civics and social studies recognize as fundamental to their instructional objectives.

### *Extracurricular Activities*

Schools may provide a forum for democratic activities and learning outside the classroom. Extracurricular activities such as athletic teams, clubs, and youth groups give students opportunities to work together toward a common goal, and often require them to select leaders and make important decisions. Students interested in theater, dance, photography, computers, and other hobbies may organize clubs for these activities, where democratic norms can be put into practice. Particularly effective at imparting democratic knowledge and skills are debate clubs, which encourage students to take an active interest in public affairs, express their opinions, and respect the views of others.

Student newspapers are also an effective and popular way to involve students in important societal issues while educating them about the role of the media. In the United

States, countrywide student competitions help promote civic knowledge. The Close Up Foundation, a civic organization with a history of successful education programs, launched the Citizen Bee competition in 1985 to encourage U.S. secondary-school students to increase their understanding of government, history, geography, economics, and current events. To prepare for the annual contest, students work with a kit of classroom-based activities and a study guide provided by Close Up. They are also expected to keep abreast of current events.

The competition itself has two parts. The first is a written examination. The second is an oral portion in which students respond to four questions. The contest begins at the school level, with the top students moving on to regional and state competitions. The winners from each state are brought to Washington, D.C., to compete in the national finals for such prizes as college scholarships. The U.S. Department of Education and the Center for Civic Education co-sponsor a similar democracy education contest, but this one involves competition among school classes, not individuals. Its focus is limited to the U.S. Constitution and Bill of Rights. Classes participating in this "We the People..." competition study specially prepared units on the history and principles of the Constitution, and then compete as teams at the district, regional, state, and national levels. Students can also learn democratic methods by creating a model of the democratic process. One of the most effective such models is student government, where students from each grade level are elected by classmates to represent them in resolving important school-related issues.

Through their involvement in campaigns, elections, and the day-to-day operations of government, students learn first-hand about the democratic process. In addition, student councils provide students with a voice in school administration—a means of influencing decisions that will affect them directly.

### *Democratic School Environment*

One important way to make the education system and school environment more democratic is to decentralize the process of school governance—and to engage more people in decision-making. Just as students should have a say in important decisions affecting them inside and outside the classroom, so should principals, teachers, parents, and others with clear interests in the policies and practices of individual schools. This objective can be accomplished in various ways. Schools may form administrator-teacher committees to make decisions on such issues as class scheduling, student testing, and classroom discipline. Parent-teacher associations may make recommendations on curriculum or school budgets. And broader governing bodies, perhaps including administrators, teachers, and parents, may oversee these and other important issues. In each case, elections can be held to determine who will serve, and meetings and forums may be called to engage a wider constituency in the issues under consideration.

In 1988, the City of Chicago embarked upon an ambitious plan to improve its school system, which had been regarded as one of the nation's most troubled. Based on the widely held belief that the city's highly centralized school system was not adequately meeting the needs of children or community, the Chicago School Reform Act provided for every public school in the city to elect a Local School Council (LSC) consisting of two teachers, six parents, two other community members, and the principal. The LSC, which makes its decisions via majority rule, is responsible for many decisions previously made by the central administration and Board of Education. Each LSC now has substantial control over its school's budget, academic program, and internal organization and priority-setting. Perhaps most significant, the LSC has the power to hire and fire the principal.

Chicago has a long way to go before these changes in structure and governance show a clear impact on student performance. Nonetheless, more than 6,000 citizens are engaged in the processes of democratic school governance: running for office, usually in contested elections; learning the procedures of orderly decision-making for a public enterprise; grappling with difficult issues and problems; and living with the consequences of their decisions. By bringing many such decisions closer to the parents, children, and teachers directly affected by them, the Chicago program also illustrates one approach to more participatory governance in an area that had long been entrusted to distant bureaucracies and politicians.

It is important to recognize that decentralization of school decision-making does not automatically make the process more democratic. Individual school heads may function in an authoritarian fashion, too. But decentralization at least creates an opportunity for sharing of authority and responsibility, for introducing more democratic forms of school governance, and for the active participation of teachers and parents. Students observing these examples of democracy in action are also apt to get a clearer understanding of how it works than those whose schools are just cogs in a vast bureaucratic wheel. Sometimes the students even participate directly. In Chicago, for example, in each high school a student representative is chosen to serve on the LSC.

## Teaching Democracy in Outside

Schools are not the only settings for democracy education. In fact, it is often through informal, community-based programs that many members of the population—especially adults—are reached. In countries emerging from totalitarianism, today's adults are products of schools that strove to denigrate democracy. Now mostly beyond the reach of the schools, these adults must rely on other means—continuing-education courses, employment-related programs, workshops, leadership seminars, radio and television, newspapers, posters, brochures, unions, and various voluntary associations—to acquaint them with democratic principles and practice.

Even where schools are involved in teaching democracy, informal programs serve as an important supplement for young people as well as adults. Understanding democracy entails more than just learning about it. It requires action. People of all ages must work to inform themselves about important issues, participate in the political process, and become involved in the affairs of their communities. Community-based programs can provide citizens with these opportunities. In addition, whereas the school-based version is usually in the hands of the state (which runs most of the schools), one of the virtues of informal democracy education is that it can come from a variety of sources under many different auspices.

The most direct community-based approach to democracy education is adult or continuing education. There is no substitute for a well-taught course on democratic government, politics, history, and citizenship, one that adequately covers democratic tradition and practice inside and outside the particular country and that makes use of some of the democratic teaching methods described earlier. Adult education is an important function in democracies, where responsible citizenship goes hand in hand with lifelong learning.

In some countries, courses for adults are offered by many different organizations, including national or local governments, public or private schools and universities, civic and community groups, churches, libraries, businesses, labor unions. These courses may be most useful when scheduled at night or on weekends to allow people with regular jobs to attend. Interactive workshops offer a more hands-on approach to democracy education.

People may be brought together in small groups to discuss current events and issues associated with life in a democracy. Group leaders or instructors may be chosen to direct the discussion, but one advantage of working in small groups is that everyone can participate in the dialogue.

Some workshops may focus on specific democratic values or skills, such as leadership or tolerance. Others may involve the study of particular institutions, such as the media or the legal system. Perhaps a judge, lawyer, or journalist could be invited to participate.

Other useful educational tools—often effective in promoting community action as well—are seminars and public forums, where members of the community can be brought together to discuss current issues and problems in front of a larger audience. If a community is having problems with crime, for example, local politicians, lawyers, judges, educators, parents, and representatives of the police force can be brought together to work on ways to keep neighborhoods safe.

### *Tools for Teaching*

Perhaps the best way to get a message out, whether it be information about candidates in an upcoming election in particular or about democratic citizenship in general, is through the dissemination of educational materials such as books, pamphlets, brochures, leaflets, and posters. For example, the distribution of brochures describing the candidates running for an upcoming election and emphasizing the importance of voting can mean a big difference in voter turnout. Libraries play an important role in a free society. By serving as a resource center and providing citizens with ready access to information on a variety of subjects, usually at little or no cost to the reader, libraries can be effective means of democracy education.

One tried and true way to learn about democracy is to read classic democratic texts—books that have significantly contributed to democratic movements throughout history. In Central America, a civic organization called Libro Libre has been making such works available in Spanish for years. Published in a series called *Classics of Democracy*, the group has presented the writings of de Tocqueville, Montesquieu, Kant, Jefferson, Madison, Lincoln, Thomas Paine, Adam Smith, Lord Acton, and Ortega y Gasset. Libro Libre has also created a series called *Democracy Today*, which focuses on more contemporary issues.

### *Role of Media*

The news media are among the most influential institutions in modern societies. Nothing reaches more people than radio, television, newspapers, and magazines, and these can be potent educational vehicles. Authoritarian and totalitarian governments understand this well and go to great lengths to control and censor their press. In democratic societies, however, the media operate free of government control; they provide coverage of important issues both in and out of the political arena and serve as a watchdog over government and other powerful institutions. Panama's Center for Democracy, formed in 1987 to help restore democracy, operates a number of excellent programs that harness the power of the media for purposes of civic education.

In conjunction with three commercial television stations, the Center has produced a series of 30-second advertisements designed to publicize its work and to convey important educational messages regarding democracy. One such spot, for example, focuses on the role of the family in a democracy—in raising responsible democratic citizens. Another reinforces the concept of community service. The Center is also working to create monthly television programs that will speak to pertinent issues and foster a better understanding of democratic institutions and principles.

The Center has conducted similar advertising campaigns by radio, which, in most cases, is less expensive and less complicated than television. The Center also conducts a weekly, hour-long radio program on topics related to the promotion of democratic values and issues of national interest. Subjects have ranged from "culture and democracy" to "community development" to "democratic education."

The most successful piece of the Center's media campaign is a monthly newspaper supplement. Inserted inside one of the leading national newspapers, this supplement serves as an advertisement for the Center and its programs and contains articles promoting democratic principles and values. Each month, the supplement focuses on a different topic, such as the history of Panama's judiciary, citizen participation in a democracy, and civic voluntarism.

### *Community Participation*

Central to any functioning democracy are the many private organizations that offer people avenues of political engagement in issues affecting their lives, their communities, and the nation at large. By joining groups such as political parties, labor unions, neighborhood associations, and religious groups, citizens are exercising their fundamental right of free association. Whatever their affiliation or focus, such organizations can serve as mediating structures between individuals and the government and give people greater leverage in their efforts to improve the life of their community. Civic groups and others involved in democracy education can help facilitate the creation of such community groups where they do not already exist.

Citizens may organize labor unions and employer groups to look out for the interests of specific occupational groups, organizations to address issues such as environmental pollution or cruelty to animals, or consumer groups to protect the public from unfair practices or unsafe products. They can create organizations to deal with such issues as public safety, services for the elderly, or the maintenance of gardens and parks. There may be a group working to improve local libraries, an organization interested in preserving a community's historical sites, or an association dedicated to finding a cure for cancer, AIDS, or other diseases.

Whatever their focus, such organizations empower citizens to take responsibility for their communities and provide them with constructive avenues of involvement. To the extent that they participate in interest groups and community organizations, citizens are also engaged in informal democracy education. They are learning firsthand about the role of private associations in a democracy and are seeing the democratic process itself being modeled within the governance of each organization.

## New Trends

Education for democracy is no quick fix. Creating the educational infrastructure and the sorts of formal and informal programs crucial to good democracy education will require hard work and a long-term commitment on the part of the government and the citizenry. There will always be a need for civic education, no matter how advanced a democratic society becomes. The longer democracy is in place in a country, the greater is the risk that citizens will take its principles, institutions, and benefits for granted. Today, some of the most innovative programs in civic education are being carried out in emerging democracies. These programs, like the recent democratic revolutions that made them possible, have helped to reawaken the interest in civic education in the more established democracies. We are now entering an exciting period when, through the sharing of the type of information contained in this document, all societies can develop education programs that ensure the growth and continued health of democracy.

Responding to students' lack of knowledge about the Australian government and the history and characteristics of that country's form of democracy, the Australian Parliament established a Parliamentary Education Office in 1987, and charged it with improving political literacy and historical awareness in the schools. That office has produced numerous materials on democracy, including two packages of curriculum materials, one for the elementary grades and one for secondary, and distributed them to all Australian schools. The "Parliament Packs," as they are called, have two components, one dealing with Australian history, the other focusing on the structure and process of Australian government. Each pack consists of a variety of teaching resources, including reference booklets, student worksheets, teachers' guides, charts, videos, and games. The teachers' guides offer detailed instructional guidance and explain how the packs can be integrated into different subject areas.

In addition to the "Parliament Packs," the Education Office has produced a variety of other materials in recent years. Among these are "junior fact sheets" on Australian government, a "Parliamentary Activity Book" for primary school students, "Parliamentary Government in Australia: A Student Guide to the Commonwealth Parliament" and "Parliament: A Two Way Street," a multi-resource kit for investigating parliament's impact on the life of young people.

Since 1988, an impressive mock election program has been operating in Arizona. Modeled after a successful program in Costa Rica, Kids Voting offers specially prepared curricula for elementary and secondary schools designed to educate students about important democratic principles and to instill in them lifelong voting habits. The program culminates with children accompanying their parents to the polls on election day and taking part in a simulated election while mom and dad participate in the real one.

Within the Kids Voting curriculum, students explore many important issues. They learn about the structure of democratic government and politics, including the roles of political parties, interest groups and the media; the qualifications for voting; the registration process; and the actual procedure that takes place at the polls. They also study the history of the expansion of suffrage and examine factors that influence voter choices and participation. When focusing on a particular election, the Kids Voting program describes the qualifications for and responsibilities of specific offices, and discusses individual candidates' views on major issues.

The most interesting aspect of the Kids Voting program is that it actually involves students going to the polls with their parents on election day and voting next to them. This not only allows children to experience how the process works, but also motivates parents themselves to vote. Kids Voting has been successful in Arizona and is being replicated in other U.S states. Ninety-five percent of Arizona s elementary- and secondary-school students have been involved in the program, and it is strongly supported by registered voters. In fact, 3 percent of Arizona voters said that Kids Voting was the only reason they took part in the last election.

### Sources of Economic Development

In the 1930s, in the midst of the Great Depression, the Skokie School, a public middle school (grades 6 8) in Winnetka, Illinois, supported a group of successful student projects called "economic enterprises." Students, with the help of the faculty, formed all kinds of "businesses." These included the Biology Bureau of Bees, which raised bees, studied their habits, and sold honey for a profit; a bank and credit union, where students could deposit and borrow money; a

Greenhouse Committee that grew flowers and vegetables and sold them for a profit; and an insurance company that insured children against loss from such mishaps as breaking dishes in the cafeteria. These activities permeated the whole school and gave both motive and application to many of the children's other studies.

A Credit Union was set up at the beginning of each school year by offering 500 shares to students at $1 each, thereby getting the "capital" they needed to operate the business. Owning these shares made the participating students owners of the business. With that capital in hand, the students managing the Credit Union would decide what interest rates to charge to children who wanted to borrow money. Student managers were also responsible, with some help from a faculty adviser, for doing the accounting for these financial transactions. A brisk business in financing cafeteria lunches for students who had forgotten theirs, or bus fare for those needing to get home, made the Credit Union's capital grow. At the year's end, the profits made by charging interest were divided among the shareholders, and the company was dissolved, to be started up again the next year.

Running the school newspaper was another source of economic "know-how." Students, in addition to serving as editors and reporters and selling subscriptions, raised money for the paper by going out into the community and soliciting advertisements from local merchants. The students also took trips to see how professional newspapers were managed and published and came back with ideas for improving their own. The enterprise taught them about the basics of newspaper financing, production, and circulation. The children participated in these groups with great enthusiasm and pleasure, and were perhaps unaware of how much they were absorbing the values and skills needed to live in a democratic society.

Through these extracurricular activities, the youngsters were learning both independence of thought and cooperation with others. They were learning tolerance, compromise, responsibility, and initiative. At the same time, they were also learning about economic organization—primarily about capitalism, the economic system that so often seems to be wedded to successful democratic governments. In the United States today, there are many organizations dedicated to the development of effective programs of economic education.

For example, the National Council on Economic Education, founded in 1949, is an important source of teacher training, educational materials, and curriculum reform. The National Council's program Economics America provides economic education for over 120,000 teachers serving eight million students each year. Among other publications, the National Council has developed "A Framework for Teaching Basic Economic Concepts with Scope and Sequence Guidelines, K-12," which is widely accepted by U.S. educators, educational policymakers, administrators, and economists.

One exercise in democracy popular in a number of countries is the Model United Nations program. This activity asks students to assume the roles of "ambassadors" from various countries to the United Nations and debate current issues on the world agenda, including the environment, economic development, conflict resolution, disarmament, and human rights. Operating within a framework of diplomacy, negotiation, and parliamentary rules, students in the Model U.N. program learn firsthand some important lessons in democracy.

The program has two basic components. First, students go through an intensive preparation process, in which they research the countries they will represent, prepare policy papers, draft resolutions, and practice rules of procedure and skills of public speaking. Second, they take part in the simulation experience itself, a process of formal debate and negotiation that can last up to five days. Model U.N. programs may take several forms. The simplest occurs within the classroom and involves 15 to 50 students. Groups of this size often simulate a particular U.N. body such as the Security Council, rather than the General Assembly. Another form of Model U.N. is the school-wide program involving some or all of the students. In this case, the simulation can concentrate on the General Assembly or other U.N. bodies. A third and more complex version is the interschool Model U.N. conference, where hundreds or even thousands of students from many schools come together.

## Future Challenges

Democracy is live, not taped. Teachers must teach about democracy so that children experience it themselves. Just as science courses need lab assignments, so educating for democracy needs hands-on encounters with the reality of self-governance. To *learn* democracy, students must *do* democracy. The question, of course, is how. Some educators believe that we should protect classrooms from controversy by insulating students from the bitter tugs-of-war between competing interest groups. These educators believe their responsibility is to define the curriculum so that interference by ordinary citizens is kept to a minimum.

As a general rule, this attempt to keep conflict out is valid; but a growing number of educators believe that teaching democracy requires allowing students to confront the diversity of opinion that surrounds them and to witness the conflicts that impinge on education. They believe that trying to keep conflict out of school will actually increase it. The alternative, they argue, is to build conflict *in*. Let's examine both approaches.

# 6

# Teaching of Reading

Extensive reading is to be possible and for it to have the desired results, texts must be well within the learners' reading competence in the foreign language. In helping beginning readers select texts that are well within their reading comfort zone, more than one or two unknown words per page might make the text too difficult for overall understanding. Intermediate learners might use the rule of hand-no more than five difficult words per page. Learners must know at least 98% of the words in a fiction text for unassisted understanding. It follows that, for extensive reading, all but advanced learners probably require texts written or adapted with the linguistic and knowledge constraints of language learners in mind.

This is all the more true with extensive reading because learners read independently, without the help of a teacher. Those teaching English are fortunate that the art of writing in English for language learners is well-developed: a great variety of high-quality language learner literature is published for learners of all ability levels. The use of easy material is controversial. There is still a pervasive view that, to accustom students to real-world reading, real-world texts should be used for extensive reading. This is to confuse the means with the end, and paradoxically to rob students of exactly the material they need to progress to the goal of reading real-world texts.

For students to be motivated to read more and study more, and to be able to ladder up as their foreign language and reading skills improve, they must be reading texts that reflect their language ability-texts they find easy and enjoyable at every step of the way. The success of extensive reading depends largely on enticing students to read. To awaken or encourage a desire to read, the texts made available should ideally be as varied as the learners who read them and the purposes for which they want to read. Books, magazines, newspapers, fiction, non-fiction, texts that inform, texts that entertain, general, specialized, light, serious. For an inside track on finding what your students are interested in reading. Varied reading material not only encourages reading, it also encourages a flexible approach to reading.

Learners are led to read for different reasons (e.g., entertainment; information; passing the time) and, consequently, in different ways (e.g., skimming; scanning; more careful reading). The principle of freedom of choice means that learners can select texts as they do in their own language, that is, they can choose texts they expect to understand, to enjoy or to learn from. Correlative to this principle, learners are also free, indeed encouraged, to stop reading anything they find to be too difficult, or that turns out not to be of interest. For students used to working with textbooks and teacher-selected texts, the freedom to choose reading material (and freedom to stop reading) may be a crucial step in experiencing foreign language reading as something personal. Further, although there may be a class or homework assignment, extensive reading puts the student in charge in other important ways.

Compliance means reading books, but other than that, the purposes and pleasures to which students put their reading are entirely their own. This encourages students to become responsible for their own learning. This is the "extensive" of extensive reading, made possible by the previous principles. The most critical element in learning to read is the amount of time spent actually reading. While most reading teachers agree with this, it may be the case that their students are not being given the opportunity or incentive to read, read, and read some more. There is no upper limit to the amount of reading that can be done, but a book a week is probably the minimum amount of reading necessary to achieve the benefits of extensive reading and to establish a reading habit.

This is a realistic target for learners of all proficiency levels, as books written for beginners and low-intermediate learners are very short. In an extensive reading approach, learners are encouraged to read for the same kinds of reasons and in the same ways as the general population of first-language readers. This sets extensive reading apart from usual classroom practice on the one hand, and reading for academic purposes on the other. One hundred percent comprehension, indeed, any particular objective level of comprehension, is not a goal. In terms of reading outcomes, the focus shifts away from comprehension achieved or knowledge gained and towards the reader's personal experience.

A reader's interaction with a text derives from the purpose for reading. In extensive reading, the learner's goal is sufficient understanding to fulfill a particular reading purpose, for example, the obtaining of information, the enjoyment of a story, or the passing of time. The learners' experience of reading the text is at the center of the extensive reading experience, just as it is in reading in everyday life.

For this reason, extensive reading is not usually followed by comprehension questions. It is an experience complete in itself. At the same time, teachers may ask students to complete follow-up activities based on their reading. The reasons for this are various: to find out what the student understood and experienced from the reading; to monitor students' attitudes toward reading; to keep track of what and how much students read; to make reading a shared experience; to link reading to other aspects of the curriculum.

For such reasons, students may be asked to do such things as write about their favorite characters, write about the best or worst book they have read, or do a dramatic reading of an exciting part of a novel. Such activities, while respecting the integrity of students' reading experiences, extend them in interesting and useful ways. When learners are reading material that is well within their linguistic ability, for personal interest, and for general rather than academic purposes, it is an incentive to reading fluency. Nuttall notes that "speed, enjoyment and comprehension are closely linked with one another". In the service of promoting reading fluency, it is as well to discourage students from using dictionaries when they come across words they don't understand.

## Extensive Reading

Extensive reading is a chance to keep reading, and thus to practice such strategies as guessing at or ignoring unknown words or passages, going for the general meaning, and being comfortable with a certain level of ambiguity. Silent, individual extensive reading contrasts with the way classroom texts are used as vehicles for teaching language or reading strategies or (in traditional approaches) translated or read aloud. It allows students to discover that reading is a personal interaction with the text, and an experience that they have responsibility for. Thus, together with freedom to choose reading material, individual silent reading can be instrumental in students discovering how foreign language reading fits into their lives. Extensive reading means learners reading at their own pace.

It can be done both in the students' own time when and where the student chooses, or inside the classroom when part or all of a classroom period is set aside for silent, self-selected reading. In the latter case, teachers may witness, as Henry describes it, "the most beautiful silence on earth, that of students engrossed in their reading". As an approach to teaching reading, extensive reading is very different from usual classroom practice. Students accustomed to wading through difficult foreign language texts might drown when suddenly plunged into a sea of simple and stimulating material. Serious-minded students, for example, in thrall of the macho maxim of foreign language reading instruction, No reading pain, no reading gain, might not understand how reading easy and interesting material can help them become better readers. Students thus need careful introduction to extensive reading.

Teachers can explain that reading extensively leads not only to gains in reading proficiency but also to overall gains in language learning. The methodology of extensive reading can be introduced, beginning with choice: students choosing what to read is an essential part of the approach. Teachers can reassure students that a general, less than 100%, understanding of what they read is appropriate for most reading purposes. It can be emphasized that there will be no test after reading. Instead, teachers are interested in the student's own personal experience of what was read-for example, was it enjoyable or interesting. The final component of orientation is practical.

Students are introduced to the library of reading materials and how it is divided into difficulty levels. It should be remembered that students unaccustomed to browsing foreign language reading material may need assistance in selecting appropriate texts of interest to them. Orientation is the first step. Guidance throughout the extensive reading experience is also needed, in light of the independence and choice extensive reading allows learners. Teachers can keep track of what and how much each student reads, and their students' reactions to what was read. Based on this information, teachers can encourage students to read as widely as possible and, as their language ability, reading ability and confidence increase, to read at progressively higher levels of difficulty.

Guidance implies a sharing of the reading experience, which leads us to the final principle of extensive reading. Teacher attitude, more than technical expertise, is what they will recall when they leave us". In short, effective extensive reading teachers are themselves readers, teaching by example the attitudes and behaviors of a reader. In Henry's words, teachers are "selling reading", and the primary way to do that is to be a reader. When students and teachers share reading, the foreign language reading classroom can be a place where teachers discuss books with students, answer their questions and make tailor-made recommendations to individual students. It can be a place where students and teachers experience together the value and pleasure to be found in the written word. The top ten principles for teaching extensive reading complement the ten principles for teaching foreign language reading offered by Williams.

## Impact of Technology Development

Language teachers are often faced with the responsibility of selecting or developing language tests for their classrooms and programs. However, deciding which testing alternatives are the most appropriate for a particular language education context can be daunting, especially given the increasing variety of instruments, procedures, and practices available for language testing. Such alternatives include not only test types with long traditions of use—such as multiple choice, matching, true-false, and fill-in-the-blank tests; cloze and dictation procedures; essay exams; and oral interviews—but also tests differing in scope and structure from these well-known options.

For example, technological developments have led to a number of new language testing formats, including computer-based and computer-adaptive tests, audiotape-based oral proficiency interviews, and web-based testing. Recent discussion of so-called "alternative assessment" has highlighted the potential usefulness of a variety of innovative testing procedures, including portfolios, self- and peer-assessment, conferencing, diaries and learning logs, and teacher checklists and observations. Increasing attention has also been given to performance-based and task-based language testing in which examinees are required to perform real-world tasks in the target language.

Language tests are simply instruments or procedures for gathering particular kinds of information, typically information having to do with students' language abilities. Tests may have a variety of formats, lengths, item types, scoring criteria, and media. We may differentiate among language test types according to such characteristics and the information provided by each. For example, a 20-item cloze test, which asks the examinee to write single-word responses to complete a reading passage, provides a very different kind of information than does a 20-item multiple choice reading comprehension test, in which the examinee has only to choose the correct responses. But deciding which of these test types is better or more appropriate is not easy.

Knowing that each uses a unique format to provide different kinds of information does not bring us much closer to selecting one or the other alternative. Indeed, attempting to select the most appropriate among available testing alternatives on the basis of their characteristics alone would be like trying to choose between a hammer, a shovel, or a screwdriver based entirely on what these tools look like. Obviously, to select the appropriate tool, we first need to have an idea about the job to be accomplished. Alone, language tests tell us little about the jobs to be accomplished in language programs and classrooms. We cannot distinguish between good or bad, appropriate or inappropriate, reliable or not reliable, valid or not valid tests based solely on characteristics of the test instruments and procedures.

Rather, we must focus instead on language assessment. Language assessment is the process of using language tests to accomplish particular jobs in language classrooms and programs. In language assessment, we first gather information in a systematic way with the help of language testing tools. For example, we may use an oral interview to gather information about students' speaking abilities, then make interpretations based on that information. Or, we may make interpretations about students' abilities to perform a range of real-world speaking tasks based on how well students perform in the oral interview. Finally, based on these interpretations, we make a decision or take action within the classroom or program. We may decide that our students need more work on oral fluency and that we should therefore devote more class time to fluency-oriented activities.

Language assessment, then, is much more than simply giving a language test; it is the entire process of test use. Indeed, the ultimate goal of language assessment is to use tests to better inform us on the decisions we make and the actions we take in language education. A number of such decisions and actions may call for the use of language tests. At the language program level, for example, we use tests to admit and place students into appropriate courses, determine the extent to which course objectives are being achieved, evaluate teacher performance, and reflect on the effectiveness of syllabus design and pedagogy.

Within the language classroom we use tests to diagnose areas of learner need or sources of learning difficulties, reflect on the effectiveness of materials and activities, encourage student involvement in the learning process, track learner development in the L2, and provide students with feedback about their language learning progress for further classroom-based applications of language tests. We may also use language tests to influence or wash back on what and how we teach; make selection decisions for entrance into universities; and certify that students have achieved a particular standard of language ability.

Although not an exhaustive list, the examples make it clear that we use language tests to accomplish a wide range of jobs in language classrooms and programs. In order to use tests in a purposeful way, language teachers first need to establish exactly which jobs language assessment should be accomplishing within a particular language education context. With the jobs of language assessment in focus, teachers will be better able to select the appropriate language testing tools and to decide how they should be used to get the jobs done. Focusing on the aims of language tests is a crucial first step toward engaging in purposeful language assessment.

However, simply knowing what decisions and actions will be based on language tests will probably not give us enough information to select the most appropriate testing tools. Indeed, the same assessment job may be accomplished in a number of different ways. Thus, in addition to knowing what job we want to accomplish with the help of a language test, we also need to give careful consideration to how the test will be used in our classrooms and programs. The test use is defined as the interrelationship between four components of the language assessment process:

a) who uses the test;

b) what information the test should provide

c) why, or for what purpose, the test is being used; and

d) what consequences the test should have.

For teachers to put together a clear idea of just how language tests should be functioning within their language classrooms and programs. Obviously, different people may want different information from tests for different purposes and with different consequences. In considering the interactions among these components of test use, teachers may realize just how differently language testing tools are being used within their particular language education contexts. However, by specifying exactly how tests are intended to be used within language classrooms and programs, language teachers should have a sound basis for evaluating and revising current assessment practice, for making the purposeful selection of appropriate language testing tools, for designating how those tools will be used, and for deciding to what extent language assessment is accomplishing the jobs it was intended to accomplish.

An important starting point for specifying intended test use is to clarify who uses the test-based information. In many language programs, teachers are the primary users of such information, because they are typically faced with making decisions and taking actions within the classroom on a daily basis. However, it is important not to overlook others who may use tests to make decisions or take actions. This list may include students, students' families, school administrators, curriculum planners, funding agencies, future employers, and university admissions officers.

Each of these potential users will naturally have particular reasons for looking at the information provided by tests, and they may require very different kinds of information from a test. Who uses test-based information will also determine how this information should be reported, as different test users may look for and understand different aspects of test score reports. Finally, different users will also attach varying degrees of importance to the outcomes of the language assessment process. Obviously, then, the range of potential test users should be carefully considered before we select and implement test instruments or procedures.

It will also be important to know who is using a test when we want to evaluate how well a test is accomplishing its intended job. In addition to knowing who uses test-based information, we need to identify exactly what information a test should provide. Although language tests may be used for a variety of reasons, and indeed, a single test may be used by different test users in very different ways, the amount and type of information provided by a language testing tool will always be limited. To ensure that the appropriate amount and type of information is gathered within the language assessment process, we first need to specify exactly what that information should be. The most direct way to specify the information needed from language tests is to think about the kinds of interpretations test users will make.

Naturally, the kinds of interpretations we make in language classrooms and programs are at least as numerous. Some common interpretations are students' global language proficiency, students' mastery of curricular objectives, students' grammatical knowledge, students' productive language abilities at the end of a course of study, the effectiveness of particular lessons, language learning objectives in need of attention within the classroom, and others.

The exact interpretations will depend on the unique circumstances associated with particular language education contexts. One crucial aspect that we should note at this stage is that interpretations are always made about someone or something. We should therefore be careful to designate who or what we are interpreting. Once we decide what interpretations we intend to make within the language assessment process, we can then specify exactly the amount and type of information needed to support these interpretations. For example, in order to support an interpretation about students' productive language abilities at the end of a course of study, we may conclude that we need information about both speaking and writing abilities.

We may also decide that we will need to have information about students' abilities to perform several different speaking tasks and writing tasks that have been taught within our language curriculum. With this specified amount and type of information, we should now be able to make a purposeful decision about the language testing tools we will need. Just as we need to specify what information testing instruments and procedures should give us, we also need to make explicit exactly what purposes we have for using tests. Once we have administered language tests, we use the resulting information to inform various decisions and actions, that is, to accomplish the jobs of assessment. It will prove helpful to give further consideration to just how we intend to use language assessment; that is, how we intend to use language tests to contribute to our overall classroom and program goals and our curricular objectives.

As test users go about gathering information and making interpretations, which then lead to decisions and actions, the use of language tests obviously affects a variety of individuals and the language classrooms and programs themselves. We should therefore specify what consequences, both positive and negative, are likely to occur as a result of the intended use of language testing tools. Individuals who might be affected by using language tests include students, parents and other family members, teachers, employers, and others involved in the assessment process. Since each of these individuals may be influenced in different ways, we should consider the potential positive and negative consequences of a test.

Additionally, the test may influence other elements of the language education context such as teaching practices, materials and activities, curricular objectives, enrollments, funding, program reputation, and so forth. For all of the individuals and program elements that may be affected by our language assessment practice, we need to ask what the worst possible consequence of using the test is, what the ideal consequence of using the test is, and what the intended consequence of using the test is.

Once we have specified the likely results of test use, we can select testing instruments and procedures that will maximize positive consequences and minimize negative consequences. Given an explicit statement about who or what the assessment practice should affect and in what ways, we can also have a basis for evaluating the actual consequences of test use. By specifying the intended uses for language tests, language teachers should be able to make well-motivated and purposeful selections of language testing instruments and procedures.

However, regardless of how carefully we select and use language testing tools, we can never predict exactly what the outcomes of the assessment process will be. To keep our language assessment practice purposeful, we therefore need to evaluate the extent to which our language testing tools are actually helping to accomplish the jobs of language assessment in our classrooms and programs. The in-depth evaluation of test use may involve a number of approaches and methods, including empirical investigations and observations.

# 7

# Preparing Teachers for Ecology Development

E. Haeckel coined the term ecology, that is the teaching of nature's budget, already in 1866, but he cannot be regarded as the founder of this discipline, since ecological problems were discussed already in Antiquity. Theophrast's works contain a vast variety of relevant examples. The history of agriculture shows, that success came only after the importance of the soil type and cultivation, the fertilizing, irrigation, the right time of sowing, and pest control had been recognized. The three-course rotation is the prime example of an ecologically useful farming in the pre-industrial society.

Different approaches to the beginning of a structured ecological research existed. C. Gesner's observations of a vegetational belting in the mountains, the discoveries made in the times of the voyages of discovery that the vegetation in different in other parts of the world. A. V. Humboldt issued a small writing pointing the way after his expedition to South America in 1807. It is called "Ideas about a Plant Geography". It contains not only a description of the vegetation, but also a vast variety of physical and chemical readings, like radiation, refraction, geological data, temperature, humidity, etc. He mapped out the vegetation of the different levels of altitude at the Chimborazo, a 6003 m high volcano that was assumed to be the highest mountain of the world in the 19th century.

The transplantation experiments performed by G. Bonnier and A. Kerner v Marilaun that they performed during the second half of the 19th century show, that habitat-specific growth types exist. We discussed the results in detail in the topic evolution. This fact alone indicates already that evolution and ecology are tightly linked and cannot be delimited exactly. They are two sides of the same coin. Evolution concentrates on a change in the genetic information, while ecology focuses more on selection and the impact of environmental factors.

Studies of this type are nowadays usually summarized under the term autecology or physioecology. The opposite of autecology is synecology. Synecology analyzes the relations between groups of organisms as well as the influences the most different factors (turn-over, productivity, nutrient cycles) have on whole biocenoses and their reactions. The behavior of the individuals or of the whole species is usually not considered.

## Ecosystem

The term ecosystem was coined by the British ecologist A. G. Tansley in 1935. He used it to define a unit that covers all organisms of a given area as well as their relationship to the inorganic environment. The organisms within an ecosystem form a biocenosis, their inanimate environment is called a habitat. The totality of all ecosystems on earth is called the biosphere. Ecosystem is an operational term, since it describes units that are less easily captured than, for example, a molecule, a cell or a species. What is defined as an ecosystem is within the discretion of the person dealing with the ecosystem. A lake, for example, a reed belt, a wood, or a cornfield can be defined and described as ecosystems. Each system can consist of a number of partial systems as can be deduced from the system theory. Which level of complexity is studied is therefore mainly dependent on practical considerations.

It is distinguished between simple and complex, between aquatic and terrestrial, between natural and human-influenced ecosystems. Among the astonishingly complex systems, i.e. those systems that are especially rich in species are tropical rain forests and coral reefs. Systems are more than just the sum of the system elements' performances. Between their elements exist numerous, often specific and usually always regulated connections. Controlled systems, in contrast, are characterized by feedbacks and thus by a high degree of stability. They are largely independent against disruptions. The higher the number of system elements and the amount of interactions with each other, the more effective fluctuations can be balanced out. But still each system has only a limited capacity. When the limit of this capacity is exceeded, then the system will not return to its original situation or will even be destroyed.

Ecosystems with only a few system elements are extremely liable to break down. Just think of a spruce monoculture or a corn field. They can only be kept in balance with the use of stabilizing, energy-consuming measures like the use of insecticides. They can, on the other hand, easily be rebuilt after complete destruction. Complex systems are very resilient, they have a large buffer capacity, but their destruction is an irreversible act. A destroyed tropical rain forest or a destroyed coral reef is lost forever.

Natural or almost natural ecosystems were able to absorb human influences for centuries, but it becomes clear that the limits of the strains on them are reached or even exceeded. Ecology has therefore during the last decades been in the public eye. Environmental protection has become a major issue of the domestic policy of many industrial nations. Many students of biology study this subject only, because they are interested in environmental issues. Ecology cannot solve political problems, it is especially unable to offer a fast aid to decision-making in order to answer short-term questions.

Changes in a human society require a knowledge about its structure, its functions, its decision-makers, the chances to alter something, and the most effective ways to initiate changes. Successes that can be achieved by organizations like Greenpeace helped considerably to create an environmental awareness among general public and politicians. Ecology is a holistic science. In ecological work, long-term experience, a detailed insight into plants, animals or microorganisms, a sound knowledge and/or mastery of physical and chemical measuring are more important than spontaneous political activity.

A co-operation between scientists of different disciplines is therefore the best way to approach the aim. A solid scientific management is necessary in order to co-ordinate the activities of all scientists participating in the project. Ecosystems change permanently. Changes and disruptions are not only caused by human activities. The evolution of organisms and their adaptation to variable environmental conditions are the main reason of the changes and thus also of the evolution of ecosystems. A sequence of differently structured systems under constant abiotic conditions is called succession.

In Central Europe, for example, certain types of forests are the most stable systems. Such a system is called a climax association. Such final links of developments exist only as long as the environmental conditions are stable. In the history of the earth, several drastic climatic changes occurred that caused the extinction of whole groups of plants and thus also to the replacement of once stable ecosystems by others.

The pre-Ice Age vegetation of Central and Northern Europe, for example, or the carboniferous swamp forests became irreversibly extinct. After the ice had gone, the landscape was inhabited again beginning in the south and slowly advancing towards the northern part of Europe. A comparison of today's Central and North European flora with that of North America shows that the European flora is far poorer in species. The variety of species of North America that was only to a small extend covered by ice the variety of species that existed before the Ice Age in Europe, too, remained. The transformation of the natural landscape into a cultivated landscape had a serious impact on all ecosystems.

Often, new ecosystems possibly worth protecting developed that could not exist under natural conditions. The *Calluna vularis* areas of the Lüneburg Heath in Germany are impressive examples. Without regular grazing by a species of German moorland sheep called Heidschnucken, these areas would soon be replaced by birch-pine-forests. Ecosystems are usually stochastic systems, on one hand, because they depend on a variety of different parameters, some of which, but never all can be captured. On the other hand are they stochastic, because they are always open systems. Their most important members, the organisms, depend on a steady supply of energy. Two conceptionally different methods to gain information about ecosystems and biocenoses exist.

1. *Stocktaking*:

– capture of (all) species of a habitat,

– determination of the percentages of the single species,

– determining of changes in the species composition as a function of time (a. during the cycle of the year, b. over a longer period of time),

– determination and capture of all those chemical and physical parameters, that the organisms depend upon.

  Stocktaking has a long tradition. Mapping of vegetation and plant geography are just two methods to be mentioned here. You can find more about stocktaking in the topic plant societies.

2. *Systems analysis*: The attempt by systems analysis is younger than stocktaking. The advent of cybernetics during the 1940th resulted in aids that help defining systems and system properties mathematically in order to develop models suitable for predictions.

Both attempts - stocktaking and systems analysis - complement each other. Only if the results gained by both methods are taken into consideration, it can be tried to understand an ecosystems and to recognize its balance, its behavior, and its sensitivity towards disruptions as well as to comprehend future developments. Only plants and a few microorganisms are able to convert light energy into chemical energy. They are therefore called producers or primary producers, P. All other organisms are consumers of the first, second or third order or dor decomposers, also called saprophytes. The life-style of producers is called autotropic, the life-style of consumers is heterotropic. A mathematical description of an ecosystem requires four basic elements:

### System Variables

System variables (vi) are a group of variables (v1, v2 ... vn) that describe the state of the system at a given time. Among them are, for example, the biomass (in gram, kilogram, or tons dry weight per square or volume unit). v1 describes thus the producers (P), v2 the consumers of the first order, v3 the consumers of the second order (carnivores, for example).

### Transfer Functions

Transfer functions (Fi) are equations that describe the material turnover of a system. They cover, for example, that part of the biomass that is lost by respiration or that part that is used to feed the organisms at the next higher trophic level. The changes of a system variable as a function of time can be described by this differential equation:

$$dvi / dt = f(v1, v2 \ldots\ldots\ldots vn, F1, F2 \ldots Fn)$$

### Inputs are Amounts of Energy

Inputs are amounts of energy or material that are available for a system, like the amount of useable sun energy, the limiting amount of minerals in the soil or the temperature as a factor determining reactions. If only the transfer functions from one trophic level to the next higher one are of interest, then the corresponding Fi becomes the input. The amount of herbivores, for example, is decisive for the amount of carnivores.

### *Proportional Factors*

Proportional factors (ci) and constant factors are unchangeable. Among them is the amount of food an animal needs per period of time. The mathematical model of a system can now be given by a set of equations that describe the flow of energy and material between the single levels. Matrix calculation is used in order to sum up sets of data and equations.

A matrix is a two-dimensional list of data, where each value can be described by its co-ordinates i and j. Matrices can be multiplied with each other. The result is a new matrix. Such a mathematical description shows, for example, which system component has a direct influence on another one. In our generalized ecosystem, this would result in an image that shows that each system component has an effect on itself, but that carnivores, for example, have no direct influence on plants.

Ecological research produces always large amounts of data. It does therefore make sense to make them suitable for the computer, i.e. to group them right from the beginning into matrices that can easily be processed by the computer. No exact sets of data can be collected for many of the required parameters. The inputs fluctuate usually very much, due to unpredictable weather conditions, for example. The number of interactions occurring in a natural ecosystem is usually bigger than those given in its model.

Animals cannot be clearly grouped into herbivores or carnivores as many of them are omnivores. But if such complications are recognized, it is relatively easy to integrate them into an existing system. Often, nevertheless, the necessary information is lacking. On the other hand, relations exist that have hardly any quantitative input. It does make sense to not consider them in the model in order to decrease the amount of work.

Until now, very few ecosystems have been described that show the properties of the system exemplarily. In Germany, there is a lake, the Plußsee in the vicinity of Plön/ Holstein, Germany, that can be cited as an example of an almost completely explored ecosystem (the work was done by the Max-Planck-Institute of Limnology at Plön, Germany). The "Solling-project" is an example of a terrestrial ecosystem, a wood, that is analyzed by researchers at the University of Göttingen, Germany.

The majority of ecologists have a solid knowledge of plant and animal species, but know only little about soil bacteria and fungi (decomposers). Hardly any data about their species composition, their population density, and their rate of multiplication under natural conditions do therefore exist. Kinetics of multiplication that were taken under lab conditions are only of partial use as those growth conditions are usually better and the rate of multiplication is thus higher than under natural conditions.

Attempts of system analysis can optimized so much that little and incomplete information becomes sufficient to make relatively apt predictions. Ecology depends on optimization processes comparable to those of projections done during elections, since all lists of data however extensive they may look represent always just a relatively small spot check of the actual not yet captured data. The accuracy of a mathematical model increases with increased complexity, while an ecosystem becomes more stable the more complex its is. Statistics shows that a systematic mistake (s) is inverse proportional to the root of the number of single measurements (1/ roots of n). The larger the amount of data, the smaller is consequently the error rate.

## Flow of Energy

The flow of energy is an essential feature of every ecosystem, since all living systems are open systems. They depend on a steady supply of energy in order to keep up the structural organization and all life-preserving functions. According to the second law of thermodynamics, each system strives for the state of highest entropy. The inversion, i.e. the coming into being of systems that are poor in entropy or are, in other words, rather well organized, requires a steady supply of energy from the surrounding. Since only plants are able to use light energy, they have a key position in every natural ecosystem.

The amount of biomass decreases drastically from one trophic level to the next one as the flow of energy is a directed process and as an optimal ten percent of the biomass of the previous tropic level can be used in the next higher one. As a consequence, four, at the most five trophic levels exist in nature. The biomass of the sum of all carnivores is always smaller than that of the herbivores, and that of the herbivores again is smaller than that of the plants. The result is a food pyramid, whose shape depends on the productivity and the species composition of the respective ecosystem.

The linear succession of the single elements (producers, consumers of the first order, ...) is called the food chain. The conditions in natural ecosystems are nevertheless mostly more complex than that, so that food web is a better way to describe the actual state. Food pyramids are usually based on biomass, not that often also on the number of species or individual organisms. More than 90 percent of the total biomass of the earth is made up by plants, only a few percent are allotted to all other groups of organisms. A comparison of the number of existing species in contrast shows that about ten times more animal than plant species exist. Under certain conditions, inverse food pyramids occur. The reason is either a spatial or a time shift in the appearance of the single system elements.

A number of animals live from dead plants or plant remnants. The biomass of living animals is therefore in some winters higher than that of the living plants. The relation is just the other way round during all other seasons. A spatial separation is typical for the deep sea, because deep sea animals live in depths were no photosynthesis and thus no plants can occur anymore. These animals live from a constant 'rain' of dead plants, almost all of them single-celled algae. In order to determine the size of the energy flow in an ecosystem, the input of energy, i.e. the amount and quality of the sunlight have to be determined first.

Those pigments that make optimal use of the available wave length of the light were selected in the course of plant evolution. Clouding over acts as a heat shield, it absorbs UV and infrared. Both are of no use for photosynthesis. Visible light is far less absorbed. The vegetation filters visible light. Bright red light does hardly reach the deeper areas, since chlorophyll and phytochrome absorb it. Germinating plants need exactly these wave lengths to control germination and growth meaning that a dense vegetation inhibits the development of new plants.

The average energy of the sun of the whole earth's surface is 2 calories (cal)/ square centimeter ($cm^2$) / minute (min). It is also called the solar constant. Seasonal fluctuations as well as differences in the exposition (southern or northern slope) cause differences in the order of magnitude. The solar energy reaches thus a mean value of 3,000 - 4,000 kilo calories (kcal)/ $m^2$ (120,672 kilo joule (KJ)/ square meter ($m^2$) / day) or 1.39 KJ/ $m^2$/ second. A part of this energy is reflected by the earth surface and is thus not available for biosynthetic processes. The remains are called the net radiation that is 1 million kcal/m$^2$/ year over the sea between 40° north and 40° south. The net radiation over land is 0.6 million kcal/ m$^2$/ year.

Evaporation and movements of the air are important factors that cause the largest part of this originally enormous amount of energy to be given off into space. Without this, the earth would rapidly overheat and life would become impossible. On the other hand, the sun energy and the resulting increase in temperature are the main reasons for the existence of climatic zones as well as of seasonal and daily fluctuations. The yearly production of biomass is an estimated 164 billion tons. A third of it is produced in the oceans, two thirds in terrestrial ecosystems.

Biomass and rate of production are two different things. The rate of production or productivity means an amount of energy bound in a certain period of time. Existing biomass alone allows only under certain conditions to determine approximate values of the turnover of energy. Each step in metabolism loses energy as heat. Therefore, it is distinguished between gross and net production. The net production is the amount that remains after the energy that is lost due to respiration has been subtracted. Among the difficulties of estimating the productivity is the fact that it can often not be distinguished whether a system (in this case a plant) is in a steady state or in a growth phase. A continuous decrease of growth results in a decrease of respiration, too, because the maintenance of structures requires lesser energy than their production.

The determination of the photosynthetic activity that is measured as the amount of emitted oxygen tells little about the productivity as a part of the oxygen is consumed by respiration and another part is required for photorespiration. The activity of photorespiration is directly correlated to the amount of available light. The single factors can be captured separately under controlled lab conditions and with a large experimental effort. From the data captured under these conditions, proportional factors can be determined. The biomass is often ascertained by measuring the amount of carbon. The factors of conversion are: 10 kcal ~ 2g dry substance ~ 1g carbon

The flow of energy is usually given as kcal/ gram (g) dry weight. Natural ecosystems are optimized for a high turnover, while ecosystems influenced by humans, especially agricultural areas, are optimized for an as high as possible rate of net production. Climax associations, like the tropical rain forest are characterized by a high productivity at an almost constant biomass. An ecosystem that is in a succession is in a very different state. A bog, for example, grows by the continuous deposition dead Sphagnum.

Only about 5 percent of all available sun energy is conserved as chemical energy in the biomass of plants. A theoretically optimal 80 percent of this energy can be used by the organisms of the next higher trophic level. In reality, the amount is usually far smaller. The major part of the biomass of woods, for example, is made up of wood that is extremely unfavourable for animal feeding. Only a few specialists can use it. The relation between gross and net production as well as the flow of energy through the system can be demonstrated especially well with the model system wood.

The available amount of light is usually no limiting factor. This is different with the supply of water. Just think of the meagre plant growth in deserts as compared to the lush vegetation of the tropics. This difference is certainly not due to light as the amount of light in the usually cloudless deserts is far larger than that of the clouded tropics. Irrigated desert areas yield a higher gross production than areas with a lower light intensity. The high losses due to respiration during warm nights lead to a higher energy consumption than in cooler areas. The rate of net production is thus lowered. This explains, why the yield per hectare of rice harvests in equatorial areas is always lower than that in temperate zones.

The net primary production may fluctuate considerably. The lowest value for 'open sea', for example, is two kcal/g, the highest is 400, the lowest net primary production of cultivated areas is 100, the highest is 4000. The values fluctuate roughly fivefold in most other types of vegetation. In order to calculate the energy fixation from the net primary production, a calorific value (kcal/g) is used. It is 4.5 (kcal/g). Grassland has the lowest value (4.0 kcal/g), while the open sea has 4.9 kcal/ g.

## Nutrient Cycles

The elements required for living systems are mostly stable. Radioisotopes play a minor role, and even the half-value period of 5770 years of 14C is much higher than the life of the average organism. As a consequence, all elements of a biosphere are preserved. All that changes is their distribution within the biosphere, some are taken to new places, others are chemically integrated into different molecular components. All changes can be described by cycles. Cycles can be drawn up for any element, but in biology, that of oxygen, carbon, nitrogen, phosphor, sulphur, as well as water are of interest. Water is no element, but a largely stable molecule that is essential for all processes of life.

Cycles can be described as systems just like the generalized ecosystem that we just got to know. Often, large pools of elements like the earth's crust, the ocean or the atmosphere are the system elements. Only a minute part of the material mills around and even less participates in the development of living systems.

### Water Cycle

The water cycle is the first to be introduced as the water supply of the earth's surface is besides the sun and the amount of energy provided by it the most important precondition of vegetation and thus also of the colonization of the earth. This known fact becomes especially impressive through satellite takings made of partially irrigated dry areas. Water can exist in three different states: solid (ice), fluid, and gaseous (vapor). It is in its fluid state at temperatures that are optimal for physiological processes. Water has a high heat storage capacity. It is moreover an ideal solvent for numerous ions.

The pH-value of underground water fluctuates between pH 3 and pH 10. It is high in the coastal areas of the oceans and still higher in the open ocean. The high alkalinity is one of the main courses of the water's high capacity for carbon dioxide that becomes carbonate/bicarbonate in the water. Only a fraction of the existing water is altered chemically. The photolysis taking part during photosynthesis makes up the main part of this fraction. The earth surface is 510 million square kilometers, 362 million of it are covered by water and 325 million square kilometers of it are open oceans.

The total amount of water is 1.5 billion square kilometers. 97 percent of it is ocean water. Only three percent is freshwater, and three quarters of it is immobile ice that makes up polar icecaps and glaciers. Its atmospheric part is lower than 0.001 percent. The amount that is available for plants has roughly the same magnitude. Atmospheric water has a fluctuating geographic distribution. It occurs mainly in the equator region. Water remains an average 9-10 days in the atmosphere, though it can return to earth after a few hours or after weeks.

The atmospheric differences in temperature and pressure are the main cause of air circulation. Above the oceans, less water comes down than enters the atmosphere (107-114 centimeter (cm)/year as compared to 116 - 124 cm/year). The situation is just the opposite above land. Here, 47 cm/year evaporate into the atmosphere, while 71 cm/year precipitate. The difference is balanced out by the draining away of surface water, especially rivers, and to a lesser extend by underground water. Two further aspects are important for a botanist: the difference in the geographic distribution of the rainfall and the part of the cycle that the plant itself takes part in.

The production of 20 tons of biomass requires 2,000 tons of water. The largest part of the water does thus pass the plant leaving it by way of transpiration. 15 of the 20 tons of fresh weight are made up by unbound water within the plant tissue. The other five are dry weight. Three of them are bound water, the rest consist of other substances.

### Oxygen Cycle

The oxygen of the atmosphere is almost completely the product of the photosynthetic activity of green plants. The oxygen content of the atmosphere increased continuously during earth history since the first occurrence of organisms that were able to split water and perform photosynthesis. The increase stopped when a balance, today's 21 percentage by volume was reached. The source of the atmospheric oxygen was mainly water and to a lesser extend other oxides. Respiration and combustion are energy-consuming processes. The end product of respiration is carbon dioxide.

The atmosphere contains about 1.3 x 1014 tons of free oxygen. The lithosphere carries even 5.5 x 1016 tons of bound oxygen, more than a hundred times more than the atmosphere. Its main part is bound as carbonates, silicates, sulfates, and other oxides. In the atmosphere, oxygen occurs mainly unbound, while the strongly ionizing cosmic radiation causes the production of ozone and atomic oxygen within the stratosphere. The ozone layer protects the biosphere effectively from short-wave UV-radiation.

Over the decades, human activities have used up increasing amounts of oxygen while carbon dioxide is set free. A decrease of free oxygen is still very unlikely. A noticeable increase in the atmosphere's concentration of carbon dioxide can nevertheless be registered. A main characteristic of the oxygen cycle is its connection with a part of the carbon cycle that plants have a key position in. The exchange rate of atmospheric oxygen is a relatively high: 2,000 years. In other words: plants produce 1/2000 of the whole atmospheric oxygen each year and the same amount of oxygen is consumed by oxidation.

The carbon dioxide of the atmosphere is completely exchanged within 300 years. The total amount of water, namely the already mentioned 1.5 billion cubic kilometer is completely split by photolysis and reproduced by oxidation within 2 million years. These values show the water cycle changes just little without the activity of plants, while the oxygen and the carbonate cycle would be altered drastically without plants.

### Carbon Cycle

Carbon is an element that occurs for the smallest part as atoms at the earth surface (carbon, diamonds). Its main part is either oxidized (carbon dioxide, carbonate/bicarbonate and a small amount of carbon monoxide) or reduced (hydrocarbons and their derivatives). The main part of the carbon of organic substances is reduced, and the fixation of carbon occurs during photosynthesis. The plants have thus a key role again. The carbon cycle is directly linked to their energy budget. Often, a subsection of the carbon cycle, the carbonate cycle, is excluded and discussed separately. This may be practical as the turnover of carbon dioxide and water-dissolved carbonate/ bicarbonate is especially easy to determine. The 14C-method helped essentially to understand the whereabouts of the carbon.

In the carbonate cycle, the reduced state of carbon is usually treated as a 'black box'. We do indeed know least about it. It contains the living substance (biomass) but also dead material that is often collectively called fossil fuel. The amount of the carbon fixed by plants is directly proportional to the gross primary production, while the amount of carbon dioxide that is set free by respiration depends on the difference between gross and net production. The main part of carbon dioxide exists as carbonate in the lithosphere. A smaller part is dissolved in the oceans.

Carbon dioxide comes to 0.03 volume percent, i.e. 300 parts per million (ppm) of the atmosphere. This is a guideline. The carbon dioxide concentration increases continuously since the late 1950th. Based on details from 1979 and 1980, the amount of carbon dioxide can be calculated up to 5.3 billion tons per year. A further 1,8 - 4.7 x 109 tons of carbon set free as the result of the destruction of the biosphere have to be added. Among this destruction is the clearing of the tropics, the destruction of the savannas as well as frequent plowing of cultivated areas. Breaking up the soil causes carbon dioxide that was produced as the result of the decomposition of organic material to surface, its absorption to humus particles does not take place, the carbon dioxide escapes into the atmosphere or is washed away into rivers and finally into the sea.

The numbers given for the atmospheric carbon dioxide concentration are average values. The concentrations may fluctuate considerably regionally and locally as a measurements close to a patch of forest show. Besides day-night fluctuations different values were captured at different heights above the soil. Some quantitative data have to be considered in order to understand the global shifts of carbon. Its total amount is 1.384 x 1018 tons, 3.9 x 1013 of which are inorganic and 1 x 1012 tons are organic. The total biomass contains 5.6 x 1012 tons of carbon, its annual gross primary production covers 1.1 - 1.2 x 1011 tons of carbon, the net primary production is 0.57 x 1011 tons of carbon. About half of the gross primary production, 0.43 x 1011 tons of carbon exactly, is made up by marine plants, usually single-celled algae. In other words: the main part of the carbon fixed by primary production is respired either directly or during the biological decomposition of dead organic material.

The lifetime of marine organisms lasts weeks, that of terrestrials years. The expanded lifetime and the associated accumulation of fixed carbon results in a decreased respiratory activity. Only 30 to 40 percent are respired. The increase in atmospheric carbon dioxide and the high percentage of the biosphere's destruction lead to the assumption that the carbon cycle is not in balance any more and that this results inevitably in an increased temperature (greenhouse effect). The reality is far more complex since only a small fraction of the carbon dioxide that is set free during combustion enters the atmosphere and remains there.

A considerable part is absorbed by the oceans. There it is used for the building up of the organisms' skeletons. The importance of this process is demonstrated by the existence of extensive chalk layers and the fact that an enhanced chalk formation has been the immediate cause for the name of a whole geological era. Hardly any hints that the annual production of biomass decreases exist despite the destruction of the vegetation by man in our time. The contrary seems to be the case, maybe because carbon dioxide has always been a limiting factor of photosynthesis. This facts should nevertheless not be overly interpreted as too high concentrations of carbon dioxide cause severe growth disorders as lab experiments showed.

The carbon turnover of terrestrial organisms can only be understood if lithosphere, surface water, atmosphere, and oceans are included. The oceans nevertheless proved to be almost closed partial cycles. The amount of carbon exchange between ocean and atmosphere are very small. Despite the large mass shifting of the surface water more commonly known as currents the water of the deep sea is hardly affected. Measurements of its 14C-content showed that below 1,500 meters depth the water remains in the Atlantic for 275 years in the same place.

### *Nitrogen Cycle*

The nitrogen cycle is far more complex than the cycles you got to know until now. 79 percent of the atmosphere consist of free nitrogen a id at least the same amount of bound nitrogen is found in the lithosphere. These large reservoirs are not immediately available for plants. In this context, microorganisms have a central role. Nitrogen fixation is the cue. Plants use nitrogen almost only as ammonium and nitrate ions. In organic materials, nitrogen is mainly required for the production of the amino-groups found in proteins or nucleic acids. Nitrate and nitrite bacteria convert the amino groups back to nitrate or nitrite. Nitrate-reducing bacteria living in the soil or in water reduce oxidized nitrogen compounds and do thus close the cycle. Nitrogen fixation and reduction do roughly balance one each other.

The production of ammonium compounds and nitrates is a limiting factor of plant growth. It is true that the lithosphere contains almost unlimited amounts of nitrates, but they occur mainly in depths that are unreachable for plant roots. For humans, too, it is uneconomic to exploit this pool. Nitrogen compounds are usually very water soluble, large amounts are therefore lost by leaching. They may, especially if occurring in addition with extensive fertilizing, accumulate in lakes or ponds and cause eutrophication. Many nitrogen fixing bacteria and blue-green algae are free-living, others live in symbiosis with plants like with the leguminosae *Cycas* or *Ginko*. The symbiotic species bind about ten times as much nitrogen as the free-living. Free-living bacteria and algae fix on average 1g/square meter/ year. The highest measured value is 20 g/square meter/ year.

The relatively high rice yields of South and South-East Asia are partly based on the occurrence of extensive populations of blue-green algae like Nostoc. They live in the shallow stagnant waters where rice cultures are cultivated. In the whole contemplation of the nitrogen cycle, global or regional changes are of secondary importance. Far more important are the local concentrations and there again mainly the concentrations in the rhizosphere of the plants. Analyses of this type have repeatedly been made.

Without the results gained from them, modern agriculture and modern forestry would not be possible. Atmospheric nitrogen is mainly inaccessible while nitrogen compounds are often very reactive and toxic. An over-fertilization does therefore often lead to degeneration phenomenons and lower yields instead to a better growth. Nitrose gases are extremely poisonous and thus a main factor in acidic rain.

### Phosphorus and Sulfur Cycles

Of these two elements plants can only use certain groups of compounds: phosphates and sulfates. In the earth's biosphere exist no gaseous and also no reducing phosphor compounds. Gaseous sulfur compounds like hydrogen sulfide or sulfur dioxide are rare and if they occur, they cause damage. It is not quite right to talk about a phosphorus and a sulfur cycle since the flow of material is almost exclusively linear at least when regarded in dimensions of hundreds or thousands of years. Only when taking human influences like fertilization into consideration, a cycle begins to evolve.

The phosphorus reservoirs are phosphorus-containing rock stratums and deposits of inorganic and organic phosphorus compounds. Phosphates are usually not or hardly water-soluble and therefore unavailable for the plant in this state. The mineral enters the ecosystems by way of a stepwise degradation usually with the aid of microorganisms. The distribution of phosphates differs very much geographically: interesting deposits occur only in Morocco. Today, the prevailing view is that enough worldwide sources of phosphorus exist to supply the agriculture also in the future with enough fertilizer. It depends on the general political climate and on the price whether this optimistic prognosis comes true. Industrial nations can easily fund the import of phosphates, developing countries cannot.

# 8

# Teaching of Plant Science

Plants (land plants, embryophytes) are of monophyletic origin from a freshwater ancestor that, if still extant, would be classified among the charophycean green algae. Plants, but not charophyceans, possess a life history involving alternation of two morphologically distinct developmentally associated bodies, sporophyte and gametophyte. Body plan evolution in plants has involved fundamental changes in the forms of both gametophyte and sporophyte and the evolutionary origin of regulatory systems that generate different body plans in sporophytes and gametophytes of the same species.

Comparative analysis, based on molecular phylogenetic information, identifies fundamental body plan features that originated during radiation of charophycean algae and were inherited by plants. These include, in probable evolutionary order: cellulosic cell wall, multicellular body, cytokinetic phragmoplast, plasmodesmata, apical meristematic cell, apical cell proliferation (branching), threedimensional tissues, asymmetric cell division, cell specialization capacity, zygote retention, and placenta.

Body plan features whose origin is linked to the dawn of plants include: multicellular sporophyte body, histogenetic apical meristem in the gametophyte body, and capacity for tissue differentiation in both sporophyte and gametophyte. Origin of a well-defined sporophytic apical stem cell and a system for its proliferation, correlated with capacity for organ production and branching, occurred sometime between the divergence of modern bryophytes and vascular plant lineages. Roots and their meristem and a multilayered tunica-corpus shoot apical meristem arose later. Regulatory genes affecting shoot meristems, which have been detected by analysis of higher plant mutants, may be relevant to understanding early plant body plan transitions. Fundamental aspects of the plant body plan are remarkably consistent within the plant kingdom and are different from metazoans.

All plants exhibit at least one form of apical meristem consisting of one or more cells that are functionally analogous to metazoan stem cells because they are histogenetic. Plants differ from animals in that the plant apical meristem has the additional capability to generate organs (leaves and stem) and reproductive organ systems (cones or flowers) throughout the life of the plant, whereas the number and form of metazoan organs are embryonically determined. Plants are often described as having a "modular construction" that allows flexibility in organ production in response to changes in environmental conditions. Plants also differ from animals in that the plant sexual life history involves an alternation of two multicellular bodies (sporophyte and gametophyte) that are morphologically different and have changed differently through time. Thus the body plans of these two life history phases have taken separate evolutionary pathways

That a simple single-celled histogenetic apical meristem appeared very early in plant evolution is suggested by the fact that this type of meristem occurs in modern plants that are considered to be early divergent and not in the green algal ancestors of plants. Early divergent plant forms include bryophytes (liverworts, hornworts, mosses), simple rootless plants considered to lack specialized food and lignified water conducting cells (vascular tissue), as well as simple vascular plants that produce spores rather than seeds. Later-appearing vascular plant groups are characterized by multicellular shoot and root apical meristems. Vascular plants differ from bryophytes in possessing two types of apical meristem, those of the shoot and root. Woody vascular plants possess two additional forms of meristematic tissues, the vascular and cork cambia.

Comparative morphology and developmental studies suggest that the apical meristems of gameto phytesysporophytes, bryophytesyvascular plants, and organsyorgan systems may be homologous, and that the more complex meristems are derived from simpler forms. Emerging data on genetic control of apical meristem development and function, derived from the study of higher plant mutants that exhibit disruption in meristems (some of which are later described) are expected to allow rigorous testing of these hypotheses.

## Microfossil Evidence

The origin of terrestrial ecosystems, including the development of modern soils and their biota and emergence of terrestrial metazoan groups, depended on the previous colonization of land by the ancestors of modern land plants. Microfossil evidence (plant spores and cellular scraps), when compared with components of modern early divergent plants and considered together with molecular systematic data, indicates that the earliest plants were morphologically similar to modern bryophytes and had appeared by the early mid-Ordovician. Later in the Paleozoic, species-rich communities of rooted vascular plants, including seed plants, appeared, producing dramatic effects on atmospheric chemistry and climate.

Molecular systematic and other evidence strongly supports the concept that the modern Kingdom Plantae, also known as Embryobiota and more informally as land plants, metaphytes, or embryophytes, is a monophyletic group composed of early divergent bryophytic groups and later-divergent groups that include some of the bryophytes and vascular plants (tracheophytes). Fossil evidence indicates the existence of several additional extinct lineages. The last common charophycean ancestor of land plants is thought to have been related to modern genus Coleochaete and order Charales, on the basis of molecular evidence.

Older beliefs that various groups of extant land plants originated independently from different algal ancestors are not supported by the recent data. Phylogeny thus anoints the charophyceans and bryophytes with a special importance in the analysis of early plant evolution and origin of fundamental developmental pathways. Comparative analysis of development in early divergent land plants and charophyceans provides insight into critical body plan and reproductive changes that supported successful radiation of land plants. Such an approach is necessary because fossil evidence bearing on the origin of the first plants is as yet fragmentary and sparse.

## Body Plan Changes in Plants

The simplest known charophycean morphology is represented by the scaly (wall-less) biflagellate unicell, Mesostigma, identified by ultrastructural and some molecular sequence data as possibly the earliest-divergent charophycean. Other taxa exhibit simple body types, unicellular nonflagellates, colonies, or unbranched filaments, composed of cells with cellulosic walls. All of the above-mentioned taxa undergo cytokinesis by furrowing (ingrowth of the cell membrane and cross wall). Phylogeny indicates that this is a plesiomorphic feature for charophyceans. None of these taxa have intercellular cytoplasmic connections, and cell division is not localized into a meristematic region.

Phylogeny suggests that the above-listed nine features were the basis for derived body plan characteristics regarded as plesiomorphic for land plants and critical to the embryophyte radiation, namely: a gametophytic body composed primarily of parenchymatous tissues having reduced surface area-to-volume ratio and generated by an apical meristemic (stem) cell having three or more cutting faces, and a multicellular sporophyte generation also possessing a histogenetic meristem and having the capacity for complex tissue differentiation.

### *Cellulosic Cell Wall*

The plant cell wall has essential morphogenetic and physiological function in that it determines cell shape and degree of resistance to cell expansion. Phylogenetic systematics and structural variation in cellulose-synthesizing complexes suggest that the cellulosic walls of the charophyceanyland plant lineage are not homologous to those of other green algae. An apomorphy of walled charophyceans (1 land plants) is the unique presence of multienzyme cellulose-synthesizing complexes arranged in rosettes of six to eight subunits at the cell membrane.

Among charophyceans, such rosettes have been found in Spirogyra, Micrasterias, Nitella, and Coleochaete. So far as is known, the cellulose-synthesizing particles of all other cellulose-producing organisms (including the bacterium Acetobacter, various algal groups that diverged earlier than green algae, and noncharophycean green algae) are oriented in rows. The geometry of cellulose complexes is directly correlated with size, shape, crystallinity, and intramolecular associations of cellulose microfibrils.

Cellulose-containing walls of protists probably evolved multiple times, originating by separate acquisition of cellulosesynthesis genes from endosymbiotic bacteria. Alteration in amino acid sequence resulting in change from plesiomorphic linear complexes to apomorphic rosettes might have occurred in as-yet-unknown bacteria or very early in the charophycean radiation. Freeze-fracture transmission electron microscopic studies, coupled with comparative analysis of cellulose synthase gene sequences of early divergent charophyceans, perhaps by using primers based on the RSW1 gene sequence from Arabidopsis, may be helpful in elucidating the origin of the charophyceanyland plant cell wall.

### *Phragmoplast*

The origin of a new mechanism of cell-wall formation during cytokinesis in charophyceans was another dramatic and pivotal event in the origin of the basic land plant body plan. A transitional early phragmoplast has been observed in some zygnemataleans, and as noted earlier, a cytokinetic system nearly identical to that of land plants is present in advanced charophyceans. At the cellular level, the transition from earlier cytokinesis by furrowing involved

- the origin of a new type of microtubule array called a phragmoplast, which consists of two sets of parallel microtubles, one set lying on each side of the forming cell wall and oriented perpendicular to the plane of wall development, and
- a change in the aggregation and binding behavior of cytokinetic vesicles containing pectinaceous wall components such that they fuse with each other, beginning at the center of the cell and moving toward the cell periphery.

The molecular basis for these two major cellular level changes is unknown.

### *Plasmodesmata*

These cell membrane-lined channels, containing protein arrays and tubular endoplasmic reticulum, provide a pathway for cytoplasmic communication between neighboring plant cells that are otherwise separated by cell walls. Plasmodesmata are thought to be dynamic, controlling the size of molecules that can pass through them by means of proteins such as myosin, actin, and possibly centrin. Because of their ability to regulate molecular traffic, plasmodesmata are considered to be critical to plant development.

Several compelling ultrastructural similarities between the primary plasmodesmata of charophyceans (Chara) and those of early divergent land plants strongly suggest that these intercellular connections are homologous and that such plasmodesmata were a feature of the earliest land plants. Plant and charophycean primary plasmodesmata are formed during cytokinesis, via enclosure of endoplasmic reticulum by coalescence of surrounding wall vesicles. However, the identity and function of plasmodesmatal proteins and the means by which they become localized is poorly understood.

So far as is known, plasmodesmata appear only in the charophyceans that also generate a phragmoplast at cytokinesis, hence it would seem likely that the phragmoplast was a necessary precursor to the evolutionary origin of primary plasmodesmata in the charophycean lineage. Plasmodesmata have not been found in zygnematalean taxa having only a rudimentary phragmoplast (Spirogyra, Zygnema, and Mougeotia).

A survey of the occurrence of primary plasmodesmata and tissue (parenchymatous organization) in eukaryotes suggests that mechanisms for intercellular communication such as plasmodesmata in plants and green and brown algae were necessary, but insufficient by themselves, for the evolution of tissues. A more complete understanding of the evolutionary steps involved in the origin of plant plasmodesmata and their functions will require identification of plasmodesma-associated proteins such as calreticulin and analysis of the timing of their evolutionary appearance, which may well have been a staged process.

*Branching*: The occurrence of branched filamentous advanced charophyceans indicates that their spindle pole organizers have acquired the ability to change angular position. Preprophase plastid migration in Coleochaete-a 90° change in the orientation of the large single chloroplast that reflects developmental change in division polarity determinants-is not known to occur in other charophyceans but is characteristic of monoplastidic apical cells of bryophytes and of sporocytes of some vascular plants.

Acquisition of branching is proposed to have been an early stage in the origin of histogenetic apical meristems in land plants; analysis of genes homologous to those identified as division site determinants in yeasts may illuminate the evolutionary origin of branching in charophyceans and histogenesis in plants.

### *Apical Meristems and Asymmetric Cell Division*

Among charophyceans, apical growth has been demonstrated only in Charales, which have a single apical cell per shoot, and in Coleochaete, where vegetative cell division is restricted to the youngest most peripheral cells. Apical cells in charophyceans have only one (Charales) or at most two (Coleochaete) cutting faces and thus generate filaments or planar cell arrays rather than threedimensional tissues. However, these charophyceans do possess histogenetic cells (capable of dividing asymmetrically and in multiple dimensions), although not located at the apex. These include nodes of charaleans and antheridial initials of Coleochaete, which generate derivatives in spiral or radial patterns. In higher plants, asymmetric division is associated with localization of the domain of function of the shoot meristemspecification gene Wuschel (WUS), which is probably a transcription regulator.

GNOM is a gene expressed during higher plant embryogenesis that is associated with asymmetric cell divisions and polarization leading to differential partitioning of cytoplasmic developmental determinants. Mutations (discordia) that disrupt asymmetrical divisions in maize leaf epidermis suggest occurrence of a gene that may influence actin-dependent guidance of phragmoplasts. A search for homologous genes in advanced charophyceans may illuminate the evolutionary origin of the plant capacity for asymmetric cell division and apical meristematic specification.

### Specialized Cells

Although specialized reproductive cells (zoospores, gametes, and zygotes) may occur in early divergent charophyceans, in this green algal class, specialized cells of the vegetative body are limited to Coleochaete and Charales. In Charales for example, smaller nodal meristematic cells and very large nondividing internodal cells are generated by asymmetric cell division. Colorless anchoring rhizoids and stipulodes, sharply pointed cells characteristic of the genus Chara, are additional examples of specialized vegetative cells. Coleochaete is defined by the presence of specialized seta cells that generate long hair-like processes and whose unusual C-shaped plastids may continuously rotate. The molecular basis for the origin of cell specialization in the charophycean lineage is unknown.

### Placenta

Evidence that chemically mediated developmental signaling between sporophyte and gametophyte phases originated in charophyceans and was inherited by land plants includes production of specialized haploid placental transfer cells near diploid cells, including zygotes of Coleochaete and embryos of land plants. Placental transfer cells are a regular feature of embryophytes, occurring at the gametophyte-sporophyte junction in all plant groups examined, from bryophytes to flowering plants. Such cells with extensive wall ingrowths and increased cell membrane surface area are thought to increase flux of photosynthate across the intergenerational junction and to have been an essential preadaptation for evolutionary origin of the plant embryo. The placenta of Coleochaete, hypothesized to be homologous to that of plants, may represent the plesiomorphic form; molecular strategies for testing this hypothesis have been proposed.

Body Composed Primarily of Tissue Generated by Apical Meristematic Cell Having Three or More Cutting Faces. The mature gametophytic and sporophytic bodies of plants, including earliest-divergent modern forms, are composed primarily of three-dimensional tissues, in contrast to charophyceans. This can be attributed to differences in the behavior of apical meristematic cells, i.e., the number of cutting faces. Mature gametophytic bodies of bryophytes are typically generated by an histogenetic apical cell having three or four cutting faces.

However, early developmental stages (sporelings, protonemata) may be filamentous, produced by an apical cell having one cutting face, or planar, in which case peripheral cells have two cutting faces, reminiscent of charophyceans. Developmental transition from peripheral apical cells having at most two cutting faces to a single apical cell having multiple cutting faces is best understood in the early divergent moss Sphagnum and is correlated with developmental appearance of preprophase bands (PPBs) of microtubules, with associated actin. In land plants, PPBs typically, although not always, mark the site where crosswall development will later commence. The microtubular components of PPBs have not been identified definitively in charophyceans.

### Multicellular Sporophyte

This feature is a unique and defining feature of plants, because (so far as is known) the diploid generation of all charophyceans is unicellular. It is thought to have been derived from the zygote stage of ancestral charophyceans via delay in meiosis and intercalation of a phase of mitotic cell division between syngamy and meiosis. Examples of sporophyte tissue differentiation that occurs in even the earliest divergent bryophytes include:

1. a protective epidermis composed of one or more layers of cells that may include tissues specialized for spore dispersal,
2. sporogenous tissues,
3. sterile support tissues located in the sporangial cavity,
4. a basal seta that may lengthen at maturity as a spore dispersal adaptation, and
5. placental tissues in close association with maternal gametophytic tissues.

Genes associated with development of homologous higher plant tissues, such as MERISTEM LAYER1, which encodes a promoter that specifies epidermal expression in meristems and young organ primordia, may have homologues in simpler sporophytes. Sporophytes of most land plants exhibit greater levels of tissue specialization than do gametophytes of the same species. This reflects an uncoupling of body plan evolution in the two phases of the plant life cycle that has persisted through time, culminating in flowering plants, whose sporophytes contain many more cell and tissue types than their gametophytes.

Genes that are influenced by changes in ploidy level, such as those recently identified by microarray technology in yeast and Ceratopteris MADS6 (a transcription factor expressed in the gametophyte but not the sporophyte), may be responsible for developmental differences in the two plant bodies and should be the target of studies aimed at dissecting the genetic basis for evolutionary uncoupling of body plans in land plants. The bryophyte sporophyte body, although thought by some to originate from single basal and apical cells, has been proposed by others to develop via subapical cell divisions; thus, a typical apical meristem is said to be absent. In addition, the bryophyte sporophyte does not proliferate organs. The genetic basis for differences in expression of meristematic activity in bryophyte sporophytes and gametophytes and between bryophyte and tracheophyte sporophytes is unknown.

## Origin of Higher Plants

Major body plan changes occurring between the divergence of modern bryophyte and vascular plant lineages were the origin of a well-defined sporophytic apical meristem that allowed the production of organs and the capacity for shoot meristem proliferation, which allowed branching of the sporophyte body in modern vascular plants (tracheophytes) and some fossil groups known as pretracheophytes. Sporophyte branching conferred increased body size, productivity, and reproductive potential as well as the capacity to continue growth if some stem cells were damaged or lost (by herbivory, for example). Multiple sporophytic growth points also permitted the specialization of branch systems to form megaphyllous leaves, cones, and flowers.

Acquisition of branching contributed to the evolutionary transition toward dominance of the sporophyte body and reduction in size and complexity of the gametophytic body that is characteristic of higher plants. A number of genes that encode proteins involved in determining and maintaining the identity of shoot meristem cells have been identified in higher plant systems and are also being sought in earlier-divergent plants. These include MADS genes that encode transcription factors expressed in meristems of the fern Ceratopteris and higher plants; KNOX and KNAT1 homeobox genes; SHOOT MERISTEMLESS (STM), which keeps meristematic cells from differentiating; PINHEADyZWILLE, a translation factor associated with meristem identity that may regulate STM expression; CLAVATA1 and 3, which oppose STM; and CLAVATA 2, encoding a receptor-like protein. Other genes are involved in the developmental transition of shoots from vegetative to reproductive function and thus also influence meristem function.

### Taxonomy and Classification

It is important that biology as a discipline develop some orderly way of handling taxonomy. Here are the levelsof classification that are commonly recognized:

- Kingdom (Eubacteria, Archaebacteria, Protista, Animalia, Fungi, Plantae)
- Division (Anthophyta = flowering plants)
- Class
- Order
- Family
- Genus
- Species Latin binomial (two names)
- Variety

Humans have been selecting various forms of particular taxa for use as food and so on. This unnatural selection process has produced plants that are unique but are still belonging to a single species. Good examples include the many cultivated subspecies of Brassica oleracea. The names below are all Latin subspecies or variety names that go with certain common vegetables. If you dissect the Latin roots of these names, we think you can see that they are just as descriptive as common names.

capitata = cabbage

acephala = kale

gemmifera = Brussels sprouts

italica = broccoli

botrytis = cauliflower

caulorapa = kohlrabi

Of course human selection created more than just subspecies! Indeed each subspecies includes many cultivated varieties or cultivars of each subspecies.

### Ways of Classification

Plant classification is one of the older pastimes in botany. Every culture, society, and religion has taken it as its duty to name and organize the plants in its area into some manageable arrangement. The arrangement at first was meant to facilitate communication between people about the plants under discussion. The earliest organizations, naturally, were based upon the uses of plants by people. Obviously some plants were useful as vegetables, others were fruits, some make great spices for other foods, some were a good source of sugar, or perhaps starch. Oils could be extracted from others. Some were good for spinning fibers into thread for clothing. Yet others were ornamental. But as is true of any classification scheme based upon human uses, there are problems of several sorts.

The uses of plants by one civilization might not be the same as those by another. Even among individuals in the same society, one person's fruit is another's animal fodder. Moreover there is the conundrum of what to do with plants that present several different uses. George W. Carver demonstrated many uses for peanuts. Henry Ford produced an automobile with body parts made of soybean products. But the worst problem with human-use classification is that it puts related organisms in different classification categories. There is no relationship between the classification system and the evolutionary pathway through which the diversity was obtained. Other early attempts at classification focused upon the form of the plant. Thus one category would be the herbs; here we use herb in its botanical sense meaning non-woody plants. A second category would be woody plants.

These plants have secondary xylem and would need to be subdivided into several sub-categories of form: shrubs, vines, and trees. Each of these categories would have to be subdivided into deciduous and evergreen. Of course whether an evergreen vine is closer related to an evergreen tree or to a deciduous vine is a very good question. And of course there are both woody and herbaceous vines. It is sounding messy. Also, we find that a natural grouping may have members in all of these "unnatural" categories. Humans have also noticed that the seasonality of plants varies and so can be another way to divide up the plants into categories. Thus in one category we have annual plants which are planted in the spring, flower that summer, and die in the fall.

Then we have the perennial plants which are planted in one year, grow vegetatively in the first year, overwinter, and then flower in each year thereafter. Nurseries like to sell annuals because they know customers will come back next year to replace them all. They sell an entire flat of annuals for a small price. Perennials are planted, and then never replaced, so nurseries place a premium price upon them. However, there is a real "gotcha" among the perennials in some nurseries, however...biennials act like perennials in the first and second year, but die all the way to the ground at the end of that second year. You will have to replace those.

Many seed catalogs are divided into annual and perennial categories. However even a casual gardener will be able to find plants of the same kind in both the annual and perennial categories. Certain species of a genus may be perennial, and other species of the same genus may be annual. It is not a natural division. Another way of dividing the plants is obvious in nursery catalogs: by climate. Tropical plants originate in areas of the world between the tropics of Cancer and Capricorn. This part of the world is very warm year-round with frost never occurring in the year. This is explained as the sun passes directly overhead on at least one day each year, and may do so for much of the year.

Tropical plants generally cannot withstand any kind of frost. Subtropical plants are slightly more hardy and can tolerate light frost but not heavy freezes. Hardy plants can tolerate frozen periods of various durations and temperatures. The hardy plants are classified on the basis of hardiness zones. In North America these range from Zone 1 (extremely cold and long winters) to Zone 10 (no frost at all). Subtropical plants survive in zones 8-10. Some hardy plants can only survive in the warmer zones (7-10) while others are tough enough to survive in zones 1 and 2!

In nursery catalogs the coldest zone for each plant is noted and gardeners are well-advised to heed those.

Connecticut is zone 6 except for the northwest corner which is zone 5. Along the shore one might experiment with some zone 7 plants if a sheltered spot is available. However, again, close relatives can be tropical plants and extremely hardy plants. This is not a natural classification scheme. One of the possible classifcation criteria above create artificial groups of virtually unrelated plants and separate out close relatives in what appear to be distinct classification categories.

Juniper is an evergreen conifer that is a tree, holly is an evergreen dicot that is a tree. These criteria also artificially separate related plants. Spruce is an evergreen woody tree, larch is a deciduous woody tree but both are conifers. So we really needed something better; this was recognized by Linnaeus and others who established the foundations of Botanical Taxonomy or what is known as Systematics.

#### *Biotic Factors*

Teachers should have a thourigh knowledge about different levels in ecology.

*Biome*: This is a region of the planet's surface that is occupied by a particular collection of ecosystems. The biome is marked by an assemblage of organisms that is dominated by particular kinds of vegetation. Most of the biomes are named after this vegetation.

*Ecosystem* : The biome is comprised of a collection of ecosystems. Each ecosystem demonstrates a particular community and its attendant environmental features and interactions. Our local biome includes upland forest, lowland forest, creek bed, pond, and meadow ecosystems. Each of these ecosystems has its own community of organisms that interact with each other and the environment.

*Community*: Each community, such as the upland forest community, holds a group of populations of various species that interact with each other. The upland forest community is dominated by canopy trees, understory shrubs, and forest-floor herbs. It is at the community level that trophic pyramids and food webs, represent the interactions. The community is dominated in numbers, biomass, and energy by the producer level of the trophic pyramid and food web.

*Population*: Each population in a community is composed of a group of individuals of a particular species that interact and that usually interbreed. In our upland forest community, there are populations of maple trees and beech trees, for example. The oak trees represent a problematic set of "species" in that they interbreed to form a single hybrid swarm population. The concept of species is often difficult to apply in the case of plants.

*Competition*: We have observed organisms in communities interact in a competitive way. The competition is generally observed for acquiring some limiting abiotic factor in the environment. So plants compete for water, light, minerals, and carbon-dioxide for example. Some plants are better-able to compete than others in a given portion of an ecosystem. These species exclude their competitors from that part of the ecosystem; this is called competitive exclusion. One example of competitive exclusion is observed between two species of Lemna (aka duckweed, an aquatic aroid).

Each species is shown to grow nicely in a chosen medium in a particular environment by itself. However when both are put into competition in that very same medium and environment, one species dominates to the detriment of the other. In this case Lemna gibba excludes the other species. Did you observe competitive exclusion in any case in the arboretum? Yes, certainly grasses were excluded in the dense shade under the canopy trees. This was obvious as we moved from the exposed grassy meadow into the upland forest.

Further evidence that light, rather than other factors, was the basis for grass being excluded was observed as grass grew nicely beneath gaps in the canopy caused by tree-fall, trails, or creek bed. A similar relationship was observed in the distribution of multiflora rose (Rosa multiflora). Arguably this might be more due to the position of seed dispersers in the environment rather than competitive exclusion. Conifers were observed struggling to survive in the shady upland forest, but these were depauperate and incapable of reproduction even after several years of growth.

*Allelopathy*: Yet, a very inhospitable place for an oak seedling is under the canopy of conifers! In the taiga biome, where pines dominate, the shade is dense, and breakdown of the crop of needles that is shed each year releases acids into the soil. These acids probably inhibit grasses and other plants from growing in a pine forest...even in most gaps! This chemical inhibition of one species by another is called allelopathy. Perhaps the most commonly known case of allelopathy is the production of growth inhibiting juglone by walnut (Juglans regia) trees.

As walnut leaves and fruits break down in the soil beneath the trees, juglone is leached out and accumulates in the soil. This chemical inhibits growth of grasses and vegetables. If your tomato plants will not produce fruits and seeds, you might check to see whether a nearby tree is a walnut...it could be a biotic factor in your garden! You will notice that it is not a competitive exclusion, rather it is allelopathic exclusion.

*Symbiosis*: Species always live together in communities, but some species interact in a much more intimate way. We call these more-intimate interactions a symbiosis (sym-= together, -bio- = life, -sis = process). There are at least four different types of direct interaction.

*Mutualism*: Mutualism exists when two species interact to the benefit of both species. Perhaps the most obvious mutualism was observed yesterday in the arboretum as we discussed lichens. Here the fungal partner (haplobiont) receives carbohydrate and more from the algal partner. The algal partner benefits from the fungal partner providing water for a terrestrial habitat for the alga. The fungal partner also decomposes the rock or other substrate and supplies released minerals for the algal partner.

Other mutualisms exist at the root-soil interface for higher plants. Legumes, such as the clover in your lawn, are in a symbiosis with Rhizobium a bacterium that can fix atmospheric nitrogen into a form that the clover can utilize. The legume supplies the carbohydrates and so on from photosynthesis to the bacterium for respiration, etc. The legume root nodule carries out repspiration at high rates and has heme-iron to mop up any extra oxygen gas, providing an anaerobic microhabitat for the Rhizobium. Other plant species live in association with fungi. The fungi live either on the surface (ectomycorrhizae) or on the inside (endomycorrhizae) of the plant roots. The plant provides photosynthate (carbohydrate, amino acids, etc.) to the fungi below ground, and the fungi decompose soil particles and detritus to provide the plant with essential minerals.

*Commensalism*: Commensalism is a symbiosis in which one partner benefits but the other gains nothing (nor loses anything) from the association. The grape vine (Vitis labrusca ) that you observed climbing a partner tree is mostly a commensalism. The grape vine benefits from the tree's support to grow into the canopy from the forest floor. The tree gets virtually nothing out of this, nor do grape vines cause much harm to the trees.

*Parasitism*: In this symbiosis, one partner benefits (parasite) at the expense of the other partner (host). In the arboretum we observed a leaf miner that spends the larval phase of its life between the two epidermal layers of a leaf, feeding upon the mesophyll cells. This feeding of the parasite reduces the productivity of the leaf in a permanent way...it is detrimental to the host. Another example of parasitism that involves grape vines is quite famous. Grape vines can be a host for the parasite aphid (Phylloxera infestans).

This was unknown to early American explorers. These people arrived in North America to lots of very-robust grape vines. They named one part of the eastern coast Vinland in honor of the vines. These plants were quite productive compared to the European grapes that the explorers knew about. However, the wine made from the American grapes had an odd unpleasant taste.

Today we would call it the "Welches" flavor...or a grape-y flavor. In the wine the flavor is called foxy flavor after the fox grapes that produce it (Vitis labrusca). French explorers were quite excited by the high yield and robust growth. They figured the off-flavor would be eliminated by moving the vines to the "superior" soil in France's vineyards. They potted some up and shipped them back to France. Indeed the grapes kept their high yield and robust growth...but alas, the flavor was still foxy. What was not clear at first was that the potted grapes from North America also brought the root aphid (Phylloxera infestans) to France.

The American grapes had evolved over the millennia in contact with this parasite and so had evolved an effective defense. Unfortunately for the French, their wine grapes (Vitis vinifera) had not evolved in contact with Phylloxera. The French grape hosts had no defense against the exotic alien aphid and the vines were dying rapidly.

Germany and Italy closed their borders and trade with France in a vain attempt to keep out the pest. Thousands of acres of vineyards were lost. The solution was found in grafting...joining the aphid-resistant rootstock of the American grape to the better-wine making French grape scion.

Other common parasite pests of plants include rusts, smuts, and scab fungal diseases, various wilts and rots by fungi and bacteria. Some of the pests have specific host/ parasite relations with particular plant species. Some have been studied extensively, most poorly. The garden pea, Pisum sativum can be a host to a particular wilt known as Fusarium. A fusarium spore lands with its chitin cell wall against the wall of a pea leaf cell. The epidermal cell of the host pea plant can detect the carbohydrates in the chitin. These carbohydrates are called elicitors. When these elicitors are detected, the pea plant responds in turn by making a phytoalexin.

The Pisum phytoalexin is called pisatin. For less-than-virile fusarium species, this pisatin prevents the growth and establishment of the fungus on the pea plant. Virile strains of Fusarium have evolved a gene producing a monooxygenase. This enzyme is produced and secreted by the Fusarium spore and it degrades the pisatin produced by the pea. This virile fusarium then continues its attack and the pea wilts and dies.

*Herbivory*: Herbivory is often treated separately from symbioses, but we prefer to think of it as just an extreme form of parasitism. Some herbivores eat just one kind of plant, so the relationship is just as specific as in the case of parasites. The difference is in what the parasite does. The herbivore literally eats the plant tissue some parasites do and some don't do that. An example of a symbiotic herbivory would include the relationships between pandas and bamboo and koalas and eucalyptus trees. It would be harder to defend as a symbiotic relationship how generalist herbivores feed in a community. Poor examples would include woodchucks, rabbits, and deer in a vegetable garden.

Plants can defend themselves mechanically from some herbivores. Species with spines or thorns or very tough bark are good examples. Cacti possess both spines and thorns. One good example is the Opuntia cactus. Its spines are long, sharp, and hard...capable of piercing through a sneaker and into your foot. Its thorns are tiny glochidia with backwards-pointing barbs; they create a wound that festers for weeks as it is almost impossible to remove them from the skin without breaking them off. Many species of arthropod larvae besides Cactoblastus feed upon plants. Our farm stores are filled with a diversity of pesticides that we can use to control various arthropod herbivores.

Plants have evolved their own batteries of pesticides. They hold these internally until an herbivore takes a bite of plant tissue...the herbivore then gets his "dose" of biochemical toxin. Chrysanthemum coccineum is known to produce the toxin pyrethrum. We now extract that poison from plants and sell it as a "safe and natural pesticide" (from a certain point of view this is an oxymoron). Other examples of plants producing pesticides include tobacco plants producing nicotine (a potent neurotoxin). Consider opium poppies that make morphine and codeine, marijuana that makes delta-9-THC, coca plants producing cocaine, peyote cactus producing mescaline, and oaks producing tannins. All of these examples include toxins that are lethal to small herbivores, such as insect larvae. For a big animal such as a human, small doses of these drugs are more "fun" than they are lethal.

*Carnivory*: Do plants ever defend themselves by "biting back?" Well, not in the strictest sense. However there are a range of plants that are competitive only in the acidic swamps of the world. The acidic water in the swamps makes soil minerals unavailable to plants. The good competitors in this environment have evolved carninvory as their competitive edge. These plants attract, capture, and digest small animals. The digestion is not for carbon supply or energy supply, rather it is to release and capture minerals such as calcium, iron, and magnesium for the plant. Because the plants digest an animal for their minerals, these plants are sometimes called carnivorous plants. If you consider the energy costs involved in digesting an animal and reabsorbing minerals from it, you realize that carnivorous plants are typically very small...shorter than a half-meter.

## Plant Succession

Finally, if plants ever alter the abiotic factors in an environment resulting in a change in the composition of the community. Rather than just be "affected" by the environment, plants do alter certain abiotic factors in some stunning ways. Of course, as a plant changes an abiotic factor that once made it competitive in a particular environment, its own change makess the species less-competitive relatively speaking. The change increases the chance that another species will replace it by improved competition.

### *Primary Succession*

Initially the earth's land surfaces were uncolonized all life was in the oceans. As organisms invaded the terrestrial environment, much of that surface was rock or gravel or sand. The first organisms to arrive in that environment are called pioneer species. These species have characteristics that permit them to survive in the virgin inhospitable surfaces.

However, many pioneer species have evolved ways to improve their growth and increase their reproductive capacity by releasing acids from their roots to degrade rocks, release minerals, reduce gravel to sand, and sand to silt, and silt to clay. In other words, the crevices where these pioneer species colonize become filled with fine mineral particles.

Detritus from the leaves of the pioneers mixes in with these mineral particles to add humus particles and to create soil. These pioneer species that colonize and establish soil are the first step in primary succession. The presence of soil created by the action of the pioneer plants, improves the chances that the pioneer species will now have to compete with other species from other areas of the environment. Areas once occupied by pioneers are quickly populated by early settler species.

As these settlers make further improvements in soil and water availability, yet other species will dominate the landscape. Each wave of replacements in succession is called a successional sere. Because this progression of seres started with bare rock or bare sand, this kind of succession is primary succession.

### *Secondary Succession*

When an area previously populated is denuded by fire or human activity, the re-establishment of new communities in that area is called secondary succession. Again, each sere alters the abiotic conditions in this area by its own growth and reproduction, making it likely that it will face further competition and be replaced by the next sere.

### *Successional Climax*

In both primary and secondary succession, the seres are replaced until a particular sere seems to be stable and to stop changing the abiotic factors. The community present in an area at the end of the succession of seres is called the climax community. This community, because of the now much-more-complex habitat and multiple seres of colonization, establishment and displacement cycles, is very diverse. Climax communities in each biome possess large arrays of species, demonstrate complicated food webs, and multidimensional trophic pyramids. Whether a succession series has reach the climax community or not is often controversial. Sometimes penultimate seres can be very long in duration and our perspective can lead us to wrong conclusions.

# 9

# Understanding Plant Physiology

A seed germinates into a plant, the plant produces a flower, part of the flower becomes a fruit, and that fruit contains a seed. The seed can be planted to start this life-cycle over again. However, it is seed-chauvinism to start here. Many plants do not reproduce via seeds at all. A seed consists of three parts: a Dormant Embryo, a Storage Tissue, and a Seed Coat. Not every seed that has evolved on this planet has precisely the same structure. In some seeds, the endosperm is retained as the storage tissue.

In other seeds, the endosperm is more or less used up to put storage chemicals into the embryo itself (commonly in the cotyledons). The *seed coat* is the three-layered outer covering. The outermost and innermost layers of the seed coat pick up a red dye used in the preparation of this sample. That dye is preferentially held by parts of the specimen that have waxy or brittle biomolecules. Cutin, suberin, lignin are three components of plant cells that pick up the red dye.

This leads to the idea that the integument has a waterproofing (cutin/suberin) function and also possibly a mechanical strengthening (lignin) function that could impede herbivory. Looking toward the inside of the seed coat, there is a bent *embryo* surrounded by some loose and light colored cells of the remaining *endosperm*. Indeed the paucity of endosperm leads us to the conclusion that much of the storage material has been moved to the embryo itself...perhaps much of that in the cotyledons. The *embryo* has an axis with a downward-pointing *radicle* including a *root apex*.

The radicle ultimately penetrates the seed coat in seed germination, branches profusely, and becomes the primary root system. In seeds with *hypogeous* germination, this hypocotyl is too short and does not grow above the soil. In species with *epigeous* germination, the hypocotyl elongates rapidly, lifting the cotyledon(s) out of the soil and into the air. The axis has two appendages, the *cotyledons*; as there are two cotyledons, *Capsella* is a dicotyledonous plant. There are two classes of flowering plants, the dicots and the monocots, and they are distinguished (in part) on the basis of the number of cotyledons found on their dormant embryos.

The part of the axis where the cotyledons attach is called a *node* because this zone of the axis does not elongate. At the extreme top of the axis is a *shoot apex*; after germination this shoot apex will elongate, and make appendages to produce the collection of stems and leaves that constitute the plant shoot.

## Structure of Seed

Inside every seed is a tiny living thing. That living thing is a little baby plant, fast asleep. A baby plant doesn't sleep the way we do. It is a different kind of sleep. We say that the plant is dormant. The word dormant comes from the Greek word dorm, which means to sleep. The baby plant stays dormant until it gets what it needs to wake up. When it wakes up, it begins to grow into a little plant called a seedling. When it does this, it uses all the soft fleshy material inside the seed for food until it is ready to make food on its own using sunlight, water, and air. There are really only three things the baby plant needs to wake up: warmth, water, and air. You might think that it needs soil, but it doesn't.

The plant will not use the chemicals found in soil for a few days or weeks, because the seed itself has everything it needs to begin growing. A baby plant need not sunlight to wake up and begin growing. In fact, many seeds begin growing underground where there is no sunlight at all. A seed only needs warmth, water, and air to wake up. Later on, it will begin to need sunlight. If there is sunlight present, the plant will use it to grow nice and healthy.

If there is no sunlight present, the plant will grow anyway, but it will grow differently. It won't be as healthy. Its stem will grow longer and longer, searching for sunlight. If it never finds the sunlight, it will eventually die, because it needs light to make food for itself once the food in the seed runs out. When the temperature is just right and there is water and air present, the baby plant begins to emerge from inside of the seed. If the temperature is not warm enough, or there is no water or air, the baby plant will stay snuggled inside its seed, fast asleep.

A baby plant will stay under its covers until it has what it needs to grow. Each of these sunflower seeds contains a baby plant, the plant's food, and a protective coating. The seeds need only warmth, water, and air to begin to grow into beautiful sunflowers. Sometimes, a baby plant sleeps for a few weeks inside its seed. Sometimes, a baby plant can sleep for years! Believe it or not, it can even sleep for thousands of years, if it must! It is amazing that inside of every seed is a baby plant waiting to awaken and become a grown plant. The baby inside the plant is called an embryo.

### *Testas*

If you have a bean seed and a sunflower seed, get them now. Look at the shells of your seeds. The shell, or coat, of a seed is called the testa. The testa protects the embryo, much like a winter coat protects a person from a cold winter's chill. Each plant's seed has a different testa.Have you ever seen the seeds that a palm tree makes? They are called coconuts, and they have a very interesting testa! Testas come in all different shapes, sizes and colors.

Seeds from some plants have thin testas, like a spring jacket. Seeds from other plants have testas that are thick and strong, like an Eskimo's coat. The walnut seed's testa is wrinkly and very strong. Coconut seed testas are strong, brown, and "furry." Corn seed testas are thin, smooth, and yellow. Lima bean testas are thin, smooth, and white. When the seed is soaked in water, such as after a warm spring rain, the testa gets waterlogged and soggy. The testa then comes off, and the sleeping embryo gets the water.

There are five main parts to the embryo in your seed: the cotyledons, the radicle, the hypocotyl, the epicotyl, and the plumule. Can you find and point to these parts on your embryo? You might not be able to see the plumule, because it might have been broken off when you pulled the seed apart. Now that you know the five main parts, you can learn a little bit about what these parts do.

*Cotyledons*: The cotyledons are the biggest part of this embryo. They have a special purpose. They provide food for the embryo once the seed opens and the embryo starts growing into a plant. To grow, the embryo needs food, and it gets that food from the cotyledons until it can start making food for itself. You will learn about how a plant makes food for itself later. It is important for you to understand that you are looking at what is called a "mature seed." That means the seed can sprout as soon as it gets the water, warmth, and air that it needs. When the seed is attached to its mother plant (remember the hilum, where it attaches to its mother?), it is not yet mature.

What's the difference between a mature seed and an immature seed? In bean seeds, one big difference is the cotyledons. When the seed is immature, its cotyledons are small, and it has an endosperm (en' doh spurm). The endosperm is food for the embryo, but the embryo cannot eat it. To help the embryo eat the food, the cotyledons absorb the endosperm. This causes the cotyledons to grow into the biggest part of the embryo. When the seed finally opens and the embryo begins to grow, the cotyledons give it the food that they have absorbed.

There are lot of different kinds of seeds. Not all of them look like bean seeds. In some seeds, the cotyledons do not absorb the endosperm right away. Instead, they start to absorb the endosperm after the seed has opened. Then, they pass the food immediately to the embryo. In those kinds of seeds, the cotyledons are much smaller than in the seed that that you have been looking at, and the endosperm is there as a separate part of the seed.

The radicle is the embryo's root. It grows into the plant's root. When the radicle grows, it makes tiny little hairs. Those hairs are little fibers that go searching for water, oxygen, and nutrients. When they find these things, they absorb them and send them into the rest of the plant. The hypocotyl will become the stem. It will elongate (that means grow longer) and go searching for light if none is present. If light is present, it doesn't have to grow as long, so it will grow thicker. If no light is present, it will elongate further, hoping that by growing longer, it will reach light.

### Plant Sprouting

The epicotyl is the top of the embryo. It holds the plumule, which will become the first true leaves of the plant. Well, when the embryo begins to grow, the cotyledons actually look like leaves as well. They are not as green as the true leaves, but they look very similar to leaves. Because of this, some call the cotyledons the first leaves of the plant. However, they are not true leaves. Plumule is a Latin word that means feather. Not all epicotyls have a plumule (leaves that have already developed). Most embryos do not have their true leaves when they are an embryo, but the bean embryo does. The bean plant already has its first true leaves, even though most plant embryos do not. Since the bean plant starts out with its true leaves already developed, that gives it a head start on growing. After all, the leaves are a vital part of the plant. They actually make food for the plant. Beans have a lot of protein.

### Germination of Seed

The seeds are carried inside the fruit by animals called *dispersers*. The animal usually feeds on the fruit (ovary wall), but "tosses" the seeds (or passes them through its digestive system). This assures that seeds end up far away from the "mother" plant, where they can develop without competition from "mom." The fruit may possess special characteristics to attract and encourage dispersal by an animal. Other seeds may be dispersed by catapult (as you observed in the arboretum walk), parachute, or other means. Once dispersed, a seed needs to germinate and grow into a new plant, eventually maturing into a reproductive adult plant.

Some seeds sprout with just water and reasonably warm temperatures. This is true of most common garden plants. Such seeds are often referred to as "seeds lacking dormancy." Wild species usually have some kind of deeper *dormancy* to avoid sprouting in late summer/fall when the seeds are dispersed. This assures that tender seedlings are not frozen at a young age, but do not appear until warm weather arrives in springtime. For these species it takes something *more than just water and warmth* to germinate.

The mother plants of our "wild" species put their embryos into dormancy by using chemicals. Perhaps in hardy plants the vast majority use *abscisic acid* to keep their embryos from germinating too early. This chemical is broken down by enzymes in the embryo over time. The enzymes have a cold temperature optimum. Thus the enzymes are not active until early winter. The abscisic acid keeps the embryo dormant from dispersal to frost. After 6 weeks at about 4°C, the optimum for the enzymes that metabolize abscisic acid, the AbA is metabolized completely. But now the cold soil keeps the embryo dormant until the warmth of spring (20°C). It is an ingenious mechanism evolved in hardy plants.

To accelerate this process artificially, seeds of wild plants can be harvested in late summer as they mature, placed in moist soil, and kept in a refrigerator (4°C) for four to six weeks. This treatment is called *stratification*. After the stratification is complete, then the plants are removed to a lighted greenhouse that is reasonably warm. This treatment is called *vernalization*. Now the seeds will have "experienced winter and spring" and will germinate.

Some other wild seeds have very *thick seed coats* that are thoroughly lignified and waterproofed. These species have evolved the ability to pass through the digestive system of an animal or survive pounding in the surf at the shore or go through a fire before they are even able to sprout. The degradation of the seed coat is called *scarification,* and this process permits water to pass through the seed coat so that the embryo can begin metabolism, elongate its radicle, and germinate. Many wild legumes, such as the Kentucky Coffee tree and the Sea Bean, have such heavy seed coats. Yet other wild seeds have an exceedingly *thin seed coat.*

The evolution of the thin coat is accompanied by dormancy that is overcome by either *light* or *darkness.* The light can penetrate the seed coat and the embryo inside can then detect whether it is deeply buried or right on the surface of the soil. Small seeds with thin seed coats often require light for germination; large seeds with thin seed coats often require darkness before they initiate germination. Think about the amount of storage materials in the seeds and the evolution of the two different signal responses will become apparent.

Some very small seeds may have a very *rudimentary embryo* (only a few cells large) and almost no storage material. The orchids you observed in the arboretum are an example. These seeds will not germinate until they are allowed to develop further. The seeds in nature are dispersed into soils that have symbiotic fungi. These fungi degrade detritus in the leaf litter and nourish the orchid embryos in the dark. Once the embryo has *"after-ripened"* to some sufficient stage, it will germinate and grow into an adult orchid plant.

Seeds of desert species (30 N and 30 S latitude) often have no winter cold signals, few animals for scarification, no fungi for nourishment or degradation, etc. These species often experience a dry season and a wet season in their environment. Not surprisingly desert species have evolved ways to ensure that their seeds sprout only when the wet seasons has arrived. Desert plants invest their seeds with *phenolic substances* that inhibit seed germination. As long as they are dry these seeds will not germinate. If there is a passing shower during the dry season, some of the phenolic is dissolved and leached out of the seed. But one shower is not enough...there is still enough phenolic left in the seed to prevent germination. After *repeated rinsing*, the phenolic is sufficiently leached out so that the seed sprouts during a *bona fide* wet season.

The biochemical mechanism for seed germination in two species: barley and lettuce. With the imbibition of water, the hormone signal in barley, *gibberellic acid* (GA), is carried from the embryo to the aleurone layer of the endosperm. The GA activates the DNA for the gene encoding alpha-amylase in the aleurone cells. Transcription and translation of that gene results in the production of alpha-amylase inside the aleurone cells. This enzyme is shipped by ER into the Golgi, sorted and packaged into vesicles, and exported through the cell membrane by exocytosis. The amylase is thus dumped into the endosperm area. There the amylase breaks down starch into the sugar maltose which is transported to the embryo. The sugar fuels respiration in the embryo so it can grow. The radicle protrudes from the seed coat, and germination is accomplished.

A similar mechanism exists in lettuce (lettuce has no aleurone and the embryo is a dicot), but the activating chemical is a pigment called *phytochrome*. This chemical exists in two different forms: Pr and Pfr. Pfr is the form of phytochrome that photoactivates the genes for amylase in lettuce; Pr is inactive. Whether a lettuce seed germinates depends on how much of each of these two forms of phytochrome is present in each cell. Typical lettuce seed batches germinate at 30-60% if placed in darkness because at least this percentage of seeds have enough Pfr to stimulate germination. If, however, you put the lettuce seeds in red light (660 nm), the red light causes all the Pr to change into Pfr.

Now 85-95% of the seeds can sprout because they all have an abundance of Pfr inside. On the other hand, if you had put lettuce seeds in far-red (730 nm) light, the far-red light would have caused all the Pfr to change into Pr. In far-red light, then, all the seeds have essentially no Pfr and so very few (0-5%) actually sprout. After plant physiologists explained this, Burpee Seed company understood why customers have trouble getting lettuce seeds to germinate well in their gardens...they tend to "bury" the seeds...they need to be exposed on the surface!

## Functions of Root

### *Water Uptake*

Roots take water from the capillary spaces between soil particles. This function is carried out by the young portions of the roots at the location of minimal cutinization of the epidermis and at maximum surface area. This location is found in the root-hair zone just proximal from the growing root tip. Thus roots take in their water through very fine roots located at the drip-line of the plant's canopy.

### *Mineral Uptake*

Root hairs are responsible for initiating and maintaining cation exchange relationships with microscopic soil particles. Here the root hair secretes hydrogen ions onto the soil particle, exchanging them for mineral ions (calcium, magnesium, iron, etc.). Then the root removes those minerals from the soil water surrounding the soil particle. You can guess what the effects are if an area has acid rain, as we do in Connecticut. Again, as this function occurs in root hairs, fertilization of trees is best accomplished by placement near the drip line of the canopy.

### Conduction of Water and Minerals

Roots contain xylem to conduct water from the soil up the plant and out through the leaves. These xylem tracheids and/or vessels are connected to others in an end-to-end design allowing soil water and minerals to be lifted up to the leaves. The evaporation of water from the leaves is the major pull of water through the xylem, but roots can also develop "root pressure" osmotically when the soil is well-watered and the plant has sufficient reserves. Evaporation of water from the soil/mineral solution bathing the leaf mesophyll cells concentrates the minerals for use by the plant as enzyme cofactors, etc. Roots also contain phloem to conduct photosynthate from the leaves to the root tips. The metabolism of roots growing in the dark of the soil is essentially dependent upon respiration. This process requires carbohydrate or other organic molecules as fuel. It also requires a supply of oxygen, which is why soil needs to drain well for good plant growth.

### Anchorage of Plant

Roots can develop secondary xylem and/or can branch profusely to provide steady anchorage for the shoot system. The architecture of a most root systems is some compromise of two fundamentally-different designs.

### Tap Root

The primary root of the plant develops in length and girth

with very little lateral branching...a carrot is a good example of a tap root. In trees this woody "post" provides excellent resistance to blowdown of the tree in wind storms. However a tap root provides little resistance to uprooting.

### *Fibrous Roots*

The primary root of the plant branches profusely interdigitating a network of fine roots in a large volume of soil particles. This design allows a plant to blow down easily but provides fabulous uprooting resistance. You can imagine that grasses that are subjected to intense grazing pressure and have evolved fibrous root systems. Again, some plants will exhibit mostly tap roots, other will have primarily a fibrous system. Yet other plants will have a compromise between a major root and several large lateral "feeder" roots with extensive fibrous roots associated with them. You can imagine that this latter plant is neither tall tree nor short herb.

The tropical Ficus root system is adapted for supporting large tropical trees through hurricanes and typhoons in spite of the poor soil found in the tropics. To gather minerals for such a large tree, the root system must cover a large, thin surface of soil, but to hold up this big tree, a fibrous system would not work. So the woody roots expand vertically forming radial walls extending out from the sides of the trunk. Human architects observing this method of support in plants adapted it for use in holding up the long walls of cathedrals; the architectural structure is known as a buttress.

This tropical Pandanus shows good development of prop roots. These diverge from stem nodes as adventitious roots, arch out over the soil, and take root and branch out in the soil some distance away form the trunk. These woody arches then support this tree against hurricanes and typhoons. Again, architects inspired by such plants modified the cathedral buttress into what are known as flying buttresses today. These are more aesthetically pleasing than the more gothic buttresses.

The tropical *Avicennia* or black mangrove is demonstrating a specialized root structure known as a pneumatophore. The black mangrove lives in a swamp of anaerobic mud sediments. In order for its root system to survive here, it must provide a pathway for oxygen to supply respiration in the roots. These pneumatophores extend above the sediments; lenticels in their bark provide entry of oxygen and interior aerenchyma provides an internal pathway for oxygen to get all the way to the root tips. In a sense, then, pneumatophores are similar to a snorkel.

### *Storage of Nutrients*

The cortex of a root is a parenchyma tissue that can store large amounts of starch, sugars, minerals, and other biomolecules for long periods of time. During the late summer and fall, trees sense the changing daylength signalling the approach of winter. They degrade the polymers in their leaves (senescence) and return the amino acids, sugars, and essential minerals, etc. to the root via the phloem. These remain in the trunk or root system all winter and are returned to the shoot in the spring sap flow. We tap this sap from maple trees, boil it down (40:1) and produce maple syrup.

## ***Apical Meristem Root***

### *Root Cap*

The very tip of the root ends in a thimble-like covering, the root cap. This cap has a column of cells in its interior that are meristematic... they divide rapidly to make more cells. The derivative cells of these divisions are pushed outward by additional divisions and ultimately will slough off from the root cap surface. These slough cells assist in reducing friction and coating the rough surfaces of soil particles through which the root must grow. In addition, the root cap cells secrete mucilage. This chemical is strongly hygroscopic (attracts and locks up moisture) forming a gel. This mucilage acts as a lubricant for penetration in the soil. Humans use mucilage for the adhesive on stamps and envelope flaps...yes you have licked the mucilage the plants use to penetrate the soil.

### *Zone of Mitosis*

Immediately proximal to the root cap is a cluster of cells that do not actively divide. This pad of cells is often called the quiescent center. These cells probably represent a reserve of cells to be recruited later in time for the meristem. As such they serve as corrections for proliferating somatic mutations. Just proximal to the quiescent center are cells that divide rapidly by mitosis, adding new cells to the length of the root. This is of course just one contribution to elongation of the root.

### *Zone of Elongation*

Just proximal to the zone of mitosis is a zone of cell elongation. In this part of the root the newly created cells expand in their long dimension to push the meristem and root cap through the soil. The addition of the cells and their elongation are the tandem contributors to root elongation. This elongation involves resculpting the wall, growth of the cell within, a coalescence of the vacuoles to form a single large vacuole, and maturation of the organelles in these cells.

### *Zone of Maturation*

As we keep moving proximally (away from the root apex), we find that the cells that are elongating are also differentiating. They are becoming distinguishable from each other. Some are destined to be typical parenchyma cells, while others will mature to be sclerenchyma cells. The difference between these cells is a matter of how much division occurs to make the cells, how much elongation occurs after the cells were made, and then how the interior of the cells matured. In the case of sclerenchyma cells the primary wall is joined by additional secondary cell wall layers that become lignified. This incorporation of lignins into the wall material makes the cell wall exceedingly hard and even brittle.

Eventually the cytoplasm is programmed for senescence and death, leaving behind an empty, hollow cell, with just the wall. As these cells are stacked end to end along the plant and the end wall degenerates, they form a kind of plumbing for the plant. These tracheary elements in the xylem will conduct water and minerals from the soil to the leaves. Yes, even dead cells can serve important functions. In addition to water and mineral conduction, the layers of xylem represent substantial support in the form of wood for tree trunks.

On the exterior of the root in the zone of maturation, the epidermal hairs elongate out into the soil particles as root hairs.These root hairs increase the surface area of the root tremendously. They assist in soil water intake. They are also critical for secreting acids onto soil particles to initiate cation exchange of soil minerals. Thus the uptake of materials occurs in these very fine young-root areas. People who do not understand this attempt to move large trees without taking the soil ball with them.

They will knock off the soil or hose it out, etc. to lighten their transplanting burden without realizing that they have doomed all the root hairs to desiccation. The tree will suffer a strong set-back shock and may even perish because of this. It helps if the moves are made in the cool of late fall or early spring.

### *Mature Root Cross Section*

The following is a list of the tissues within that root:

- *Root Hairs* - cell extensions of epidermis increase absorptive surface
- *Epidermis* - water and non-selective mineral intake via root hairs
- *Cortex* - storage parenchyma (starch, sugar, etc.)
- *Endodermis* - selective mineral pump
- *Pericycle* - origin of lateral roots in young areas, bark on older roots of woody species Vascular Cylinder
    - *Phloem* - conducts nutrients from leaves
    - (*Cambium* - makes wood-woody plants only)
    - *Xylem* - conducts minerals and water up

## FUNCTIONS OF STEM

### *Support of Leaf Display*

The stem must be strong enough and flexible enough to position the leaves in the sunlight to optimize the photosynthesis of the plant.

### *Support of Flower Display*

The stem must put the flowers into a correct (usually visible) position to attract the appropriate pollinators. The stem must be able to support the weight of some perching pollinators. In the case of wind pollination, the flower must be positioned properly for male parts to be upwind and up-gravity from the female parts.

### *Support of Fruit Display*

A plant must be able to support its load of developing fruit. For wind-dispersed fruits and seeds, getting the fruits up to the wind exposure is critical. For animal-dispersed fruits and seeds, the stem must position the fruit for best display or best attachment to the animal parts.

### *Conduct water and minerals up from soil*

The flow of xylem continues from root to the leaves via the stem. The stem must not only conduct minerals and water up through the plant, but it must distribute it to all elements in the shoot system (leaves, flowers, fruits, etc.).

### *Conduct water and nutrients*

Sugars and amino acids from photosynthesis in the leaf are conducted by the phloem in the stem to the rest of the plant. This flow will be upwards from leaf to apical bud, to flower, or to fruit as well as downwards from leaf to root.

### *Photosynthesis*

In some species, such as cacti, the stem is the primary site of photosynthesis. In cacti, the leaves are converted to non-green spines, and the branches to non-green areoles.

### Storage of water, etc

In the stems of cacti, in underground stems such as in potato, and in the swollen hypocotyl of radish, water can be stored. Of course this water needs to be protected from herbivory in desert situations.

### Defense

Desert plants have evolved spines (from leaves) and glochidia (from lateral buds) to mechanically protect the stems from herbivory. The stem must position these appendages and support them sufficiently for them to function. In other species, such as Lophophora williamsii, the peyote cactus, the stem posesses mescaline or other potent chemistry to deter and/or kill herbivores.

### Anchorage

Especially in vines, stems provide anchorage functions. This anchorage can be accomplished by: twining as in morning glory, by the formation of adventitious roots as in poison ivy, or by the formation of "suction cups" as in Virginia creeper.

### Shoot System

The stem and its shoot system originate at the shoot apical meristem. The shoot apical meristem also has appendages: leaf primordia. There is no cap on the shoot tip; it grows into the air and does not need protection from abrasion. However the leaf primordia tend to arch over the zone of cell division to protect this tender meristematic tissue from herbivory and desiccation.

### Mature Dicot Stem

The protoderm matures to become the epidermal system.

The ground meristem matures into cortex (just under the epidermis) and pith (just inside a ring of vascular bundles). Each vascular bundle consists of four layers. Toward the cortex the bundle may show a layer of fibers. These are sometimes called phloem fibers and the individual cells are highly elongate having expanded by intrusive growth. Some individual fiber cells can be in the range of meters in length. These fibers have been removed from stems, spun into thread, and woven into fabric. The fibers of flax were treated this way right here in Willimantic.

Moving interior to the fibers, we can find the functional primary phloem. Here sieve tube elements conduct water and sugars and amino acids from the leaves to the rest of the plant. The sieve tube cells are alive, but lack nuclei and other organelles. They are comparable to red blood cells in humans. However, unlike RBCs, phloem sieve tube elements can live for years. This ability is provided by adjacent companion cells. The companion cells have complex cytoplasm with mature organelles and provide the metabolic and homeostatic needs of the sieve tube elements through plasmodesmata... cytoplasmic strands that connect between these two types of cells.

The presence of two cell types with vastly different appearance gives the functional phloem area a superficially "messy" look. A closer examination reveals some regular patterns in the distribution of the various cell types in phloem tissue. The next layer toward the pith is the vascular cambium (aka cambium). These cells are arranged in regular rows and columns like an accountant's spreadsheet. These cells are meristematic and divide mitotically to produce additional secondary xylem and secondary phloem in woody plants. This layer may be absent in some non-woody species...such as grasses.

The innermost layer of the vascular bundle is the *primary xylem*. This tissue conducts water and soil minerals up the stem from the roots. Like human skin cells, most of these xylem elements are dead at functional maturity. The tracheids and possibly vessels of the plant stem serve as plumbing. They lack cytoplasm altogether at maturity...the last act of the cytoplasm in the developing tracheary element is to digest its own cytoplasm and sometimes also its end walls to form the pipes through which the water and minerals are conducted.

### *Anatomy of Monocot Stem*

Monocots such as grasses are put together in a similar fashion. The epidermis serves window and gas exchange functions, the ground parenchyma may perform photosynthesis and/or storage functions. The stem of sugar cane is famous in that regard. The vascular bundles are typically not arranged in a single circlar array. Rather a range of concentric rings of various diameters are found. Careless authors will call the arrangement "scattered;" that is a pet peeve of mine. Just because we humans are too simple minded to look more carefully to see the pattern, we lazily call it "scattered" as if they are whimsically arranged.

## FUCNTIONS OF LEAVES

### *Photosynthesis*

The leaf in typical plants is the site of photosynthesis for the plant. The overall equation for this complex process appears deceptively simple:

$$CO_2 + H_2O \rightarrow O_2 + CH_2O$$

### *Evaporative Cooling*

The flow of water in the xylem continues from root to the leaves via the stem. The water leaves the xylem in the leaf and evaporates from the internal cells into the atmosphere. This evaporation accomplishes three functions...it cools the leaf which might otherwise bake in the hot sun, it draws more water up through the xylem in the stem below, and it concentrates the mineral nutrients supplied by the root.

### *Reducing desiccation*

To help restrict water losses to manageable rates, the leaf epidermis layers are usually coated in *cutin* a waxy substance. The layer of this wax over the epidermis is sometimes called *cuticle*. The *Carnauba* palm leaves have a very heavy layer of cuticle. We boil up the leaves in a vat, strain out the cooked leaves, let the vat cool and remove the floating wax. This carnauba wax is used directly as an automotive polish, with dye added it can be used as shoe polish, if pure enough if can be used as a mold release for candy making. The epidermis may have *epidermal hairs* to provide a boundary layer of humid air over the leaf surface to retard evaporation. Virtually all leaves have stomata, openings, in the epidermal layers to regulate water loss and gas exchange.

### *Export nutrients*

Sugars and amino acids from photosynthesis in the leaf are loaded into its phloem and exported to the rest of the plant. This flow will be upwards from leaf to apical bud, to flower, or to fruit as well as downwards from leaf to stem to root.

### *Storage of water, etc*

In the leaves of many succulent plants, water can be stored. Of course this water needs to be protected from herbivory, particularly in desert situations.

### *Defense*

Leaves have evolved into spines in cacti and other plants to mechanically protect the plant from herbivory. In other species, such as *Erythoxylon coca* and *Cannabis sativa,* the leaf produces potent chemistry to deter and/or kill herbivores. In these two examples the drugs are cocaine and delta-9-tetrahydrocannabinol, respectively.

### *Anchorage*

As you have observed in peas in the laboratory, leaves sometimes produce *tendrils* at their tips. These can assist a plant climb obstacles in the environment or other plants to gain a competitive edge.

The leaf originates as a leaf primordium at the shoot apical meristem. This origin is *exogenous* rather than *endogenous* as in lateral roots. The photomicrograph shows that these primordia are attached to stem at zones of little elongation growth known as *nodes*. The leaf primordia tend to arch over the zone of cell division in the stem to protect this tender meristematic tissue from herbivory and desiccation.

### *Structure of a Leaf*

Although the leaf primordium is cylindrical at first, just as stem and root, it later develops marginal growth to produce a flattened organ. Intercalary growth of the cells in this tiny primordium then expands the blade to full-size. Because most leaves have a particular final size, we call them *determinate*. Stem and root are *indeterminate* in size for many species. The leaf of *Welwitschia* is indeterminate in size it just keeps elongating throughout the life of the plant.

Anatomically, the protoderm matures to become the epidermal system. The epidermis facing the sun is called the *upper epidermis* and it has mostly window functions (permit light entry, prevent gas and water loss). The epidermis facing the soil is called the *lower epidermis*; it is fitted with openings called *stomata* for gas exchange. Specialized *guard cells* in the epidermis regulate the size of the stomata and thereby control water loss and gas exchange. Of course clearly the one epidermis becomes the other as it wraps around the edge of the leaf, so the separate names are somewhat artificial. However, some leaves have a far higher density of stomata in the lower epidermis than in the upper. Thus while the epidermis is a single continuous layer, it is asymmetric in many species.

The ground meristem matures into mesophyll. The mesophyll is divided into two layers; just under the upper epidermis is the *palisade mesophyll*. This layer is responsible for most of the photosynthesis as it has the best exposure and the densest population of chloroplasts in each cell. The lower layer of mesophyll is the *spongy mesophyll*. This layer also carries out photosynthesis, but it is in the shadow of the palisade layer, so the spongy layer is more important for evaporative cooling and gas exchange than it is for photosynthesis.

Evaporation occurs into the *gas space* between all the cells of the mesophyll. This evaporation of water cools all of these interior surfaces. The provascular tissue in leaves forms *xylem and phloem* as expected. The xylem which was on the interior of the stem, connects outward to the leaf and therefore ends up facing the upper epidermis and palisade layer. The phloem which was toward the exterior of the stem, connects outward to the leaf and therefore ends up facing the spongy mesophyll and lower epidermis.

The xylem and phloem are packaged into veins and ramify into a complex network in the leaf blade. This network is called veination. In dicot leaves the veination is often called *netted* because the network is quite intricately interconnected to form a net. In many monocot leaves, most of the veins run *parallel* to each other. But of course, close inspection will reveal vascular cross-connections between these parallel veins in monocots. But it is also true that some monocots do not show parallel veination at all well in their leaves.

Leaves come in many sizes and shapes. Sometimes there are many shapes of leaves on the same plant; *Sassafras* for example has four leaf shapes on the same plant! On this plant, leaves can have lobes, so the blade can be ovate, left-handed mitten, right-handed mitten, and tri-lobate. In many plants the leaves are *simple* (one blade per petiole). In other species, the leaves are *compound* (more than one blade per petiole). Some species have the multiple blades attached to the end of the petiole (*palmately* compound), others have them attached along the edges of the petiole (*pinnately* compound). Yet other leaves have no petiole at all (*sessile*).

Leaves are attached to the stem at a position called the node. The number of leaves that attach to the node determine the *leaf arrangement*. If only one leaf is attached at each node, the arrangement is *alternate*. If two leaves attach at a node, they are in an *opposite* arrangement. If more than two leaves attach at the node, then the leaves are *whorled*. The many shapes, compositions, and arrangements of leaves permit a taxonomist to use leaves as important characteristics to distinguish plant species.

However a leaf shape, composition, and arrangement is more likely to lead to a genus identification than it is to lead to a specific identification. Leaves also vary in lifespan. In *deciduous* species, the leaves last less than a single year, and in the autumn these all fall off, leaving the bare stems. In *evergreen* species, the leaves last more than one year, so there never is a time that the plant has bare stems. However, even in these evergreen species, older leaves change color and fall from the branches each season, and often in autumn.

A walk under some pine trees will reveal much leaf-litter to you. The color change is a result of biochemical breakdown of materials in the aging leaves. The subunits of those materials are loaded in the phloem of the leaf and are transported to the rest of the plant for use in the next season. The plant is not recycling hydrocarbons in this *senescence* process; it is recycling mineral and other nutrients. The chlorophyll binding proteins have much nitrogen that needs to be retained. The chlorophyll contains nitrogen in the porphyrin ring system, and a Magnesium ion that is also worthy of retention. So the green color disappears.

Anthocyanins and carotenoid pigments are hydrocarbons or less...so they are dispensable to a plant. So *abscission* is initiated as the last of the minerals have been mined from the leaf. An abscission zone in the petiole of the leaf produces the enzyme, pectinase, and the cells come "unglued" to each other in this layer of the petiole. The weight of the blade then causes the separation of leaf from the stem.

### Pathways of Photosynthesis

The history of discovery and the photo-electronic-chemi-osmotic processes involved in the so-called "light reactions" is interesting. The parallelisms between respiration and photosynthesis are worthy of emphasis.You should be aware of the fundamental arrow-direction differences, and the three distinct phases shared by the two reaction pathways:

- Glycolysis and sucrose synthesis are both enzymatic processes occuring in the cytosol. They involve the structural relationship between a half-sugar and a whole sugar.
- The Krebs and Calvin cycles are a cyclic set of enzymatic reactions occuring in the cytoplasm of an endosymbiont and process carbon as carbon dioxide.
- The light reactions and electron transport chain are electronic in function, using a set of membrane-bound carriers. These carriers are heme-iron and quinone/ polyphenol electron/proton handlers. They pump protons across the inner membrane to conserve energy. That energy is trapped in chemi-osmotic ATP synthesis as the protons are leaked back into the cytosol of the endosymbiont (organelle).

Here is an even simpler comparative diagram:

Respiration:

$$CH_2O + O_2 \bullet CO_2 + H_2O + ATP$$

Photosynthesis:

$$CO2 + H_2O + light \bullet CH_2O + O_2$$

The two reaction systems are basically the reverse of each other. One undoes the other in plants. Since plants do not eat to supply their energy needs, the plant must do enough photosynthesis to meet its needs for maintenance, growth, and reproduction while compensating for losses due to respiration both night and day. There are two important differences between the pathways outlined above...making them not quite the reverse of each other.

One critical difference is the role of NADPH rather than NADH between the electronic and enzymatic portions. If these two very similar reducing agents were identical, it would be possible to use the Krebs Cycle to drive the Calvin Cycle. This would make the Calvin Cycle truly a "dark reaction," but NADH produced by the Krebs cycle has insufficient reducing power to drive the Calvin Cycle reactions.

The phosphorylated NADPH does have this power, so the Calvin Cycle is dependent upon the light reactions of photosynthesis, and so occurs only in the light. The second critical difference between the pathways is an energy conversion solution. While the respiration pathway yields energy trapped in the form of a phosphate bond in ATP, photosynthesis requires the harnessing of energy in the form of light. The energy transduction step is a very important fundamental difference; this is where chlorophyll becomes a critical part of photosynthesis. It is this very special molecule that has the capacity to absorb light energy while hanging onto its electron pool long enough to drive an electron transport system.

The heterocyclic ring system with conjugated double-bonds (an electron cloud) in association with a magnesium ion (another large electron cloud) provides a large volume in which electrons can be boosted for this energy-harnessing transduction to occur. Because of this critical feature of chlorophyll in photosynthesis, we can write the simplest form of photosynthesis as:

Photosynthesis:

$$CO_2 + H_2O \rightarrow O_2 + CH_2O$$

## LIGHT REACTIONS

In prerequisite courses you have studied the light reactions quite extensively. First, light has wave properties. the length of the wave determines the energy and color of the light. Human vision and photosynthesis cover the range of wavelengths from 400 to 700 nanometers. The high-energy end of this spectrum is the shorter wavelength purple light at 400 nm. The rest of the rainbow and decreasing energy follows as wavelengths increase to the lowest-energy red light at 700 nm. Light also has photon, particle, properties.

Light intensity is measured as photon flux density: photons per square meter per second. Sunlight provides a plant with tremendous energy. Plants tap small amounts of energy in some very interesting biochemistry, releasing in each step some energy in the form of heat. So photosynthesis obeys the Second Law of Thermodynamics in every way. Because short-wavelength light has higher energy, you might expect plants to use that part of the solar spectrum for photosynthesis.

However, evolution would not favor that approach...much of the light energy from the sun would be lost to photosynthesis because the photons would lack sufficient energy to drive the reactions. So it turns out the the reaction center pigments, P680 and P700, are chlorophyll pigments absorbing light maximally at 680 and 700 nanometers...in the low-energy red-end of the visible spectrum. Of course if plants could only absorb 680 and 700 nanometer light, they would be missing a lot of light.

So evolution has provided chlorophyll a with a range of other pigments, antenna pigments, that absorb higher-energy wavelengths and pass the absorbed energy on to chlorophyll a. Thus plants can utilize light from every wavelength in the visible spectrum from 400 to 700 nm. This is best observed by examining the action spectrum for a particular plant:

Obviously plants will be using less of this light and reflecting more of this color to our eyes. Plants look green. But green still drives photosynthesis! So obviously then, a plant must have more than green pigments that assist in photosynthesis. Other pigments must trap light...for example green light...and pass the energy on to chlorophyll. Also you might notice that wavelengths outside the range of the graph shorter than 400 nm might be able to drive photosynthesis!

Indeed the near-ultraviolet wavelengths can be absorbed and the energy is sufficient to survive the transfer to chlorophyll P680 and P700. However, wavelengths longer than 700 nm appear to be unable to drive photosynthesis. The wavelength is too long, the energy content of the photons too low, to be able to excite the electrons of P680 or P700. Between 680 and 700 nm, the light can probably drive just one of the two photosystems and so efficiency drops rapidly in this range of wavelengths.

### *Function of Light Intensity*

Here you can see that respiration rates do not change with photon flux density, it is not a light-driven pathway. You can also see that photosynthesis cannot be driven in the dark (0 PFD) and increases with increasing light intensity. Because Respiration and photosynthesis basically undo each other, there is a place on this graph where the respiration and photosynthesis lines cross. The photon flux density at this particular point is called the compensation point because the two processes compensate for each other. At densities below this point, the plant is dying.

At densities above this point, the plant can be growing and reproducing. At the compensation point, the plant is "breaking even" in terms of producing carbohydrate and using it. There are two lines representing photosynthesis in two different plants...a fern and corn. Obviously ferns are shade-tolerant and can grow and thive in darker conditions (compensation point is lower for ferns). They are also "scorched" by intense sunlight probably by oxygen free-radicals produced by excessive photolysis. But this brings up the interesting question of why our government spends research dollars on crop photosynthesis but does not fund much research on the really efficient photosynthesis of ferns or other shade-tolerant species.

Clearly as we must farm more intensely, finding ways to crop under orchard trees would be one way to maximize food production. Getting the fern photosynthesis adaptations into corn might be worth a bit of research. Obviously light energy drives photosynthesis. We have learned above that photosynthesis is not a single step, but in fact consists of two major groups of reactions. One set of reactions is largely electronic and light drives the electrons through an electron transport system coupled to phosphorylation of ATP. This has been called the "light reactions." The other half of photosynthesis has been called the "dark reactions" even though they never have and do NOT occur at night.

Some people want to call the dark reactions the "carbon fixation reactions" even though carbon fixation is just one chemical reaction of many in that pathway. So we have a hard time choosing names for this second group of reactions. Suffice it to say that these are largely enzymatic reactions rather than electronic, and they occur in the stroma rather than in the thylakoid. The light is funneled to two photosystems with the red-absorbing reaction center pigments P680 and P700. These two reaction center pigments are chlorophyll a molecules that are different in absorption maxima due to the way they are held by the chlorophyll binding proteins. You isolated those in cellular and molecular biology classes by doing electrophoresis.

You will notice that the light funnel consists of antenna pigments that absorb different colors of light. By having P680 and P700 absorbing such long-wavelength/low-energy light, evolution has provided a pathway for photosynthesis to harvest virtually the entire visible spectrum! Next you notice that light excites P680 and shoots electrons up to Phaeophytin. The huge jump in energy is not achieved by magic... we did not violate the second law of thermodynamics.

The loss of electrons allows P680 to split a water molecule and replace its electrons. This action releases protons and oxygen gas. The protons participate in the electron transport chain and the coupled photophosphorylation steps. Thus water is the source of the electrons used in photosynthesis. Now, where do these electrons go? What is the amazing part about how chlorophyll works?

Chlorophyll is an amphipathic molecule. It has a polar head and a non-polar tail. This allows it to bind to chlorophyll binding proteins in the thylakoid membranes and to interface with the similarly amphipathic phospholipid bilayer. The "head" portion of chlorophyll is a porphyrin ring system. It is polar because of unshared electron pairs on oxygen and nitrogen atoms that comprise the porphyrin system.

The bonding pattern in the ring system is resonant, notice the notation with alternating single and double bonds. This provides a large cloud of resonating electrons that are shared collectively over the large surface of the head of the chlorophyll molecule. Adding a nice big cloud of electrons and holding them in place is a chelated Magnesium atom. Metals like magnesium have wonderful ability to lose electrons or gain electrons; they have multiple valence states. The surrounding tetrapyrrole ring system just enhances this ability to gain and lose electrons.

So the large vertical arrows in the "z" scheme of the light reactions indicate the movement of electrons into the large electron cloud at the head of chlorophyll. From here, Phaeophytin picks the electrons up and passes them in turn to Q, cytochrome b, plastoquinone, cytochrome f, and plastocyanin. These electron transport molecules are embedded in the thylakoid membrane. Protons from photolysis are shuttled by plastoquinone from the stroma into the thylakoid lumen.

This accumulation of protons represents a conservation of energy. The leakage of protons through an ATP synthase from lumen to stroma releases that energy which is trapped in the phosphate bond in ATP. So the electron transport system of the light reactions is coupled to phosphorylation; this is termed photophosphorylation. The electrons then move to P700 to replace electrons boosted by light and passed to X, ferredoxin, and then either NADP or cytochrome b6. Again, the boosing light can be just about any wavelength in the visible spectrum because the energy is sufficent to transfer from antenna pigments to P700 and leave some energy to satisfy the second law of thermodynamics.

If ferredoxin passes the electron to NADP, the NADP is joined by some of the protons that have returned to the stroma. This produces a supply of NADPH for the carbon fixation reactions. Because these electrons do not stay in the light reactions, we call this non-cyclic flow. Since an electron can cycle through this pathway indefinitely, producing ATP from the energy lost along the ETS, a plant cell can produce any ratio that is needed of NADPH and ATP.

# 10

# Assessment of Language Learners

Some readers may not be familiar with the terms used to describe assessment and testing practices. An assessment portfolio is the systematic collection and evaluation of student work measured against predetermined scoring criteria, such as scoring guides, rubrics, checklists, or rating scales. Because the contents of portfolios are scored using specific criteria, the use of assessment portfolios is considered criterion-referenced assessment. Portfolios can provide a continuous picture of student progress, rather than a snapshot of student achievement that single-occasion tests provide.

Depending on school or district requirements, portfolios can include performance-based assessments, such as writing samples that illustrate different genres; solutions to math problems that show problem-solving ability; lab reports demonstrating an understanding of a scientific approach; or social studies research reports demonstrating the ability to use multiple sources. In some cases, multiple drafts of student work showing improvements are included. Portfolios can also contain information about students' educational backgrounds. In addition, portfolios might include scores on commercially-developed, nationally norm-referenced tests, such as the Iowa Test of Basic Skills (ITBS) and the California Test of Basic Skills (CTBS).

Portfolios may also include results of criterion-referenced measures such as the Maryland School Performance Assessment Program (MSPAP). This information can be collected for each student in folders or boxes, or electronically on a computer diskette or CD-ROM. Portfolios provide a broader picture of student achievement than do tests alone, and can include a great deal of information that shows what students know and can do on a variety of measures. Assessment portfolios can include not only the results of commercially-developed, norm-referenced tests or single-occasion, criterion-referenced tests, but also additional measures of student achievement such as writing samples or lab reports.

In contrast, students take norm-referenced, standardized tests, such as the ITBS on a single occasion, and are then compared to other students in their cohort nationwide. The information provided to the state, district, school, or parents is a single score, or a score broken down into thematic subparts. Many educators find that scores from single-occasion, standardized tests such as the ITBS provide them with little information to help them improve student learning.

Moreover, English language learners are often not included when these tests are given. Criterion-referenced tests are developed by stakeholders within a particular educational community to compare student performance with predetermined learning outcomes. In Maryland, for example, the learning outcomes for the MSPAP were established by content-area teacher teams from around Maryland, with goals to be met by the year 2000. The MSPAP tests, given to third, fifth, and eighth grade students each year, are scored by Maryland teachers based on rubrics and other scoring criteria.

Tests such as the MSPAP provide schools with richer information for school improvement teams at each school than do norm-referenced tests, but individual student results are not given to teachers, students, or parents. Like some norm-referenced tests, the results of the MSPAP are aggregated by school and do not predict how well an individual student will perform in the classroom. Likewise, information about English language learners is not disaggregated. Portfolios are inclusive of all students. Because many schools are concerned about equity or adherence to government regulations, including English language learners in assessment programs is an increasing priority.

Assessment portfolios can be compiled for all students, including English language learners. These students are often excluded from norm-referenced and criterion-referenced testing programs because of their lack of proficiency in English. Many districts have policies that exclude English language learners from taking these exams for one to three years after their arrival in the school system, or until a certain English proficiency level is reached. Meanwhile, these same measures act as gatekeepers that can exclude students from educational opportunities such as gifted and talented programs, magnet school participation.

As a result, exclusion from a system-wide testing program deprives English language learners from access to important educational opportunities that are based upon the results. In contrast, all students, including English language learners, can be included in assessment portfolios, since this involves collecting samples of student work and scoring them according to predetermined criteria. Portfolios demonstrate student learning and achievement more accurately than single test scores do. Assessment portfolio systems can be designed to assess knowledge gained or skills developed in any content area. Portfolios provide a rich source of information because they can include documentation of a student's educational background; multiple examples of student work; and scores on norm-referenced or criterion-referenced tests, along with standardized English proficiency tests like the Woodcock-Muñoz Language Survey.

Moreover, entries in a portfolio are more likely to be representative of the effects of instruction than are commercially-developed, norm-referenced test scores. Portfolios, therefore, can be used by educators to determine how well an educational program works. In addition, an assessment portfolio system is one of the few assessment approaches that accommodate a wide range of learner abilities. The fact that portfolios can demonstrate growth is particularly important for English language learners. Because portfolios are designed to be inclusive and contain authentic descriptions of what students can do, even English language learners at the beginning levels of English proficiency can participate.

For example, these students can write a story or perform a math or science activity and then be judged according to scoring criteria. Single-occasion, norm-referenced, and criterion-referenced tests may be linguistically and culturally biased, and they do not distinguish between levels of knowledge and proficiency in English. For example, one writing prompt used in a state performance assessment asks students to write a business letter to the school principal making suggestions about a recreation centre that is being built, including what students would do there, what equipment might be needed, and who might work in the centre.

Students are also asked to write about what benefit the student and others might gain from the centre. A newly arrived immigrant student may not know what a recreation centre is, and therefore could not do well on this assessment even though the student may be able to write a coherent argument about another topic.

Perhaps the most compelling reason for schools to implement assessment portfolios is that they can improve student learning. By using assessment portfolios, teachers can include students in the process of setting educational goals and developing scoring criteria in the form of rubrics, checklists, and rating scales.

Students can become involved in assessing their own and others' work based on the scoring criteria, thus focusing on the academic goals they are trying to achieve. A growing body of literature indicates that self-assessment and self-regulation of learning are powerful forces that help students improve their learning.

One research demonstrates the efficacy of self-assessment, advocates of assessment portfolios and school reform enthusiastically support portfolios. Data from large-scale assessment portfolio programs also indicate that the use of portfolios can result in improved student learning. For example, an evaluation of Kentucky's portfolio assessment program conducted by researchers at Western Michigan University found that students in Kentucky were writing more and doing more group work as a result of the new portfolio program.

Teachers and other stakeholders reported "almost unanimously" that student writing had improved in

Kentucky. Portfolios can promote improved teaching. When teachers decide to put into practice an assessment portfolio system in their school or classroom, this decision involves in-depth, often time-consuming discussions about what assessment information they need and how they can obtain it. These discussions lead teachers to the development of scoring criteria such as rubrics, checklists, and rating scales.

Teachers clarify their goals for their classes as the scoring criteria emerge. Once goals and expectations are defined, teachers often try to align their scoring criteria to their goals for their students. This process naturally leads teachers to evaluate their teaching methods and helps them move toward a more learner-centered teaching model. In such classrooms, students have greater control over their own learning, and teachers act more as facilitators than as dispensers of knowledge. Thus, portfolios not only ensure that teachers will encourage students to use self-assessment to focus student attention on goals and expectations, but encourage teachers to evaluate their own instructional practices as well.

For example, in schools in Vermont that have elected to participate in the statewide writing portfolio assessment, all teachers at the fifth and eighth grade levels have been involved in professional development on the use of writing portfolios. Many teachers have been trained intensively so that the inter-rater reliability (the reliability of scoring among evaluators) is improved.

Geof Hewitt, a writing assessment consultant for the state, noted that the program not only provides state officials with a richer understanding of how well students write, but has the added effect of improving teaching and learning because of the information that teachers and students gain by reviewing the portfolios.

After studying Vermont's portfolio assessment program, researchers from the Rand Corporation concluded that the effects of portfolio assessment on instruction were "substantial and positive". In fact, Vermont's state-wide assessment system was the only state system that was considered a "model" by FairTest evaluators, because it is based on state standards, relies very little on multiple choice items, and includes portfolios.

The use of portfolios with English language learners increases the ability of schools to be more accountable for all students. At the state and district levels, assessment information is often collected to ensure that schools are addressing the needs of all their learners, including English language learners.

When schools have the array of information that portfolios can provide, and individual students or groups of students perform poorly, the causes can be studied and solutions sought. Without this kind of information, schools are not held accountable for all their learners.

Traditional testing practices have sidestepped accountability issues with English language learners because of various types of exclusion policies and the cultural bias of tests. In contrast, assessment portfolio systems can be designed to include a range of measures that allow English language learners with varying levels of language proficiency to demonstrate what they know and can do, and can include examples of learning tasks that connect not only to classroom content, but also to students' cultural backgrounds.

Finally, the increased interaction between students and teachers contributes to a more accurate understanding of students' knowledge and skills. Portfolios can help schools create a shared vision for student learning, aligned to standards. The process of developing a portfolio system that includes English language learners helps teachers, administrators, parents, students, and other stakeholders create a common vision of what students should know and be able to do as a result of their coursework.

When ESL and bilingual program teachers contribute to developing this vision, the assessment process will take into account important issues in second language acquisition. For example, when assessing content knowledge, teachers can look beyond language errors alone and focus on how well students demonstrate an understanding of concepts.

By clearly articulating learning goals and the criteria upon which to assess students' attainment of the goals, school systems help create a shared vision of the purpose and intended outcomes of education. Once goals have been clarified, school systems can identify, select, and create assessments and scoring criteria that measure the attainment of those goals. Benchmarks, or samples of student work that represent a specific level of performance, can be identified to allow educators to have a common understanding of the quality of student work required for the specific performance levels. Goals for student learning can also be directly linked to state content and performance standards. As a result of the standards-based reform movement, a number of states and school districts have revised their curricula, but few districts have implemented content standards appropriately for English language learners or measured attainment of the standards with valid and reliable assessments.

To do so, both language and content standards should be represented in both ESL and content area curricula. The school district in San Diego, California is one of the first in the United States to assess all students using an assessment portfolio system that includes English language learners and is based on a shared vision of standards-based education. In California, 1996-97 school year, this system measures the progress of students in a program that aligns the district's English language development (ELD) program and the English language arts (ELA) standards. The new assessment system was implemented in the 1997-98 school year and now assesses all students district-wide in grades K-12, including those who speak a first language other than English.

## Assessment Portfolios

Assessment portfolio systems have lower reliability and comparability than norm-referenced tests. Assessment portfolios are not without challenges as school- or district-wide assessment tools. First, state education agencies (SEAs) report that there is general public resistance to performance-based testing, because it is perceived to diminish the accountability of schools and districts.

The public has become accustomed to single scores, like those used to describe the results of standardized, norm-referenced tests, such as the CTBS. Single scores are comparable across schools and districts, and from one year to the next. However, many performance-based tests, including some portfolio systems, do not easily or meaningfully translate into a single score or set of scores that can be readily compared. Because some schools and districts report the results of performance-based tests descriptively, using words rather than a numerical score, stakeholders sometimes feel that the school system is less accountable for individual students.

Furthermore, it is difficult to implement assessment portfolio systems to meet the reliability requirements that many school systems want. However, assessment portfolio systems can also be designed with the single-score requirement in mind. For example, inter-rater agreement on Vermont's writing portfolios improved when scores on five writing subsections were averaged into a single score. When assessment portfolio results are translated into numerical scores, the benefit of richer information about student learning is lost.

If possible, providing both kinds of scores will help stakeholders use the information for a variety of purposes. Standardized testing conditions are more difficult to ensure with portfolios than with norm-referenced tests. Some states and school districts are prevented from putting into place performance-based assessment programs that include portfolios by state legislatures mandating the use of norm-referenced tests. When using assessment portfolios, the conditions under which student work samples are produced may vary. There may be differences, for example, in the amount of support teachers provide to students, the amount of time students are allowed to spend on developing portfolio samples, and the extent to which student work is augmented by support from external sources, such as teachers, peers, parents, and tutors.

These factors have raised questions about the validity of judgments on student competence based on portfolio work. In contrast, when norm-referenced tests with multiple-choice formats are used, variance due to testing conditions and teacher bias can be minimized. Contrary to perceptions, however, standardized testing conditions can be implemented for specific contributions to a portfolio, such as a writing sample. In Vermont, for example, the statewide writing prompt is administered to all students in grades four and eight at the same time across the state, and educators receive training to learn which testing accommodations are permissible and which are not.

Implementing a portfolio assessment system inclusive of English language learners can be costly. One major hurdle in developing an assessment portfolio system is the cost of developing and implementing it. According to a Rand Corporation report on the cost of science performance assessments in large-scale testing programs, the cost of using performance tests is three to ten times higher than using multiple-choice tests. However, science may be the most expensive content area for which to develop performance tasks because of the use of manipulatives.

Designing, implementing, and scoring any assessment measure is labour intensive, and assessment portfolio samples are no exception. Practitioners invest a substantial amount of time to align the assessment tasks with the curriculum and develop the scoring criteria and tools (rubrics, checklists, and rating scales). When English language learners are included, teachers need to understand the implications of second language acquisition and incorporate this understanding into their evaluation of English language learners' portfolios. Good rubrics help teachers do this, but additional professional development costs are incurred in the process.

Costs accrue throughout the development phase and into the implementation phase for both assessment portfolios and standardized tests. The only cost incurred that is not also incurred by standardized tests is that of scoring the portfolio samples. State legislatures and school boards often inaccurately believe that standardized tests are less costly to design and administer. When a school system purchases a contract with a standardized testing company, and a one-time cost is incurred, this may be true. However, many states and districts now purchase tailor-made tests, the design and implementation of which are quite costly. Still, getting state legislatures and school boards to agree to the additional costs involved in scoring an assessment portfolio system that includes English language learners can be difficult.

One way to address the issue of cost, as demonstrated in Fairfax County, Virginia, is to view assessment and staff development as integrally linked and to integrate the cost of portfolio development into the professional development budget. When teachers begin to develop a portfolio program, the only real expense they incur is the cost of their time. If the portfolio program is started slowly and built steadily, portfolios can actually be less expensive than buying standardized tests. Scoring portfolios is more difficult than scoring norm-referenced multiple choice tests. Portfolios pose a scoring dilemma for two reasons. First, developing and using scoring criteria require labour-intensive staff discussion and training.

Educators must keep second language acquisition principles in mind as the scoring criteria are developed, to ensure that the criteria are valid and reliable for all students, including English language learners. When appropriate, content rather than language form should be the focus of assessment portfolio systems that include English language learners. If the school uses assessment portfolios in addition to traditional testing, finding the time to score the portfolios can be particularly burdensome for teachers. Fortunately, some teachers and schools have devised innovative ways to solve this problem.

One ESL teacher, Anne Bingley, has an effective method for handling the time constraints of portfolio assessment and at the same time providing her students with more individualized attention than she herself could give. She invites English-speaking community members into her classroom to interview individual students and to review and rate their portfolios on simple criteria regarding the written content, the oral presentation, and the visual presentation. The second reason that portfolios can be difficult to score, mentioned earlier, is that developing inter-rater reliability among raters, usually teachers, requires intensive staff development and is time consuming.

In Fairfax County, Virginia, a district-wide assessment portfolio system is used to assess and monitor the progress of all English language learners within the ESL program. Teachers in Fairfax County have received ongoing staff development on the use and scoring of the portfolio samples. In most cases, teams of scorers, who have received training, score writing samples based upon predetermined criteria. A subset of the portfolios is usually reviewed by more than one scorer until the desired inter-rater reliability level is reached.

Although the process is more time-consuming than the process of scoring a single-occasion, norm-referenced test would be, the staff development efforts needed to train teachers to use portfolios and to develop inter-rater reliability have an unexpected benefit. They result in having teachers who share a common vision of what student achievement in the particular subject looks like. Teachers decide together what benchmarks to use for assessing student work. School staff throughout the system are in close agreement regarding the outcomes being sought and the criteria being used to measure student performance, enabling stakeholders to share a common goal. Most norm-referenced and criterion-referenced tests cannot achieve this result.

Professional development is an integral part of any assessment reform effort and should be an ongoing activity throughout the duration of a portfolio project. Teachers should first be made aware of the benefits of assessment portfolios so that they become convinced that it is an attractive alternative to their current testing system, especially because portfolios require more work initially than standardized tests.

Highlighting the advantages and challenges of assessment portfolio systems would be an excellent introduction. Professional development activities should show teachers how to embed portfolio assessment into their instructional programs, so they can plan for assessment opportunities as they plan their instruction. As a result of such planning, the use of assessment portfolios will be more manageable.

Professional development plans should also include a description of the teaching strategies that lead students to take responsibility for and reflect on their own learning. Effective teaching strategies that encourage this include heterogeneous grouping, cooperative learning, student-centered instruction, the integration of language and content instruction, overt teaching of learning strategies, and peer coaching and collaboration among teachers.

In addition, all teachers working with students learning English should understand the process of second language acquisition and its impact on learning. If possible, individual portfolio users should initiate a school-wide project to develop assessment portfolios with the aim of creating a shared vision of the goals for student achievement. In this way, students and teachers alike will understand what is expected of them. Another important feature of a professional development plan for the effective use of assessment portfolios is to provide opportunities for members of an educational community to discuss student work together. This enables teachers to improve assessment practices, learn how to work better with individual students, and improve the curriculum.

The process itself also helps to establish a culture of shared learning within the school community. Additionally, teachers should be instructed in developing scoring criteria that accurately reflect their course content and trained to use those criteria to score student work equitably. Finally, the professional development plan should provide teachers with enough scoring opportunities to enable them to score portfolio samples reliably and to choose samples of student work that are representative of a specific level of performance.

This process, known as benchmarking, also gives the educators who score the portfolios a common understanding of what the scoring criteria look like in terms of student work. Improved teaching results from the staff development that prepares teachers to use and score portfolios equitably. The hidden benefit of such teacher training is that it also prepares teachers to work with an increasingly diverse student population. More importantly, it leads to improved student achievement.

Many districts across the United States have implemented school- and district-wide assessment portfolio systems for their English language learners, including Calexico, California; San Diego, California; Arling-ton County, Virginia; Fairfax County, Virginia; and Prince William County, Virginia.

Stakeholders within the school and district, including those responsible for English language learners, decide what assessment information is needed and how that information can be provided. A group of teachers agree to lead the development of the portfolio program. The lead group of teachers, including ESL and bilingual education teachers, administrators, and parents decide on the range of products to be included in the assessment portfolio program.

The group decides upon common goals for student learning and performance and how students will be assessed, develops scoring rubrics and checklists, and agrees upon standards of performance to be attained. If possible, benchmarks that exemplify levels of student achievement should be articulated, including benchmarks for English language learners. Study the effects of the assessment portfolio program on English language learners in particular, to determine whether improved information about these students is available as a result of portfolio implementation.

## Context-based Approach

Developing students' strategies for handling unknown words has always been one of the principal challenges of English reading classes. In China, the usual approach to this challenge is to have students read only passages in which every word is known, or else allow them to consult a bilingual dictionary or the teacher for the definition of every new word in the passage. The drawbacks of this approach are obvious. Too much dictionary work can kill all interest in reading and even interfere with comprehension, because readers become more concerned with individual words and less aware of the context which gives them meaning.

It also results in very slow and inefficient reading . Guessing vocabulary from context is the most frequent way to discover the meaning of new words. Honeyfield stresses the importance of context by arguing that even with a functional vocabulary of the 3,000 most frequently occurring items in English, learners will still not know approximately 20 percent of the items they will encounter in an unsimplified text. Researchers agree that to learn words in context and not in isolation is an effective vocabulary learning strategy.

A word used in different contexts may have different meanings; thus, simply learning the definitions of a word without examples of where and when the word occurs will not help learners to fully understand its meaning. Learning an isolated list of words without reference to the context is merely a memorization exercise which makes it difficult for learners to use the words in spoken and written language.

Looking at the context in which the word appears seems to be the best way of learning vocabulary. Good readers also take advantage of their background knowledge in processing the context and in creating expectations about the kind of vocabulary that will occur in the reading. There are four assumptions in a context-based approach to acquiring vocabulary:

1. Drawing inferences from what we observe is fundamental to thinking, and the same principle can be used in the reading process. Schema theory suggests that the knowledge we have is organized into interrelated patterns. These patterns are constructed from our previous experiences and guide us as to what we might expect to encounter in a new context. Making use of what we know in order to understand the unknown is a common practice in our daily lives. For instance, if we are in a building and observe that someone is entering folding a wet umbrella, we will infer that it is raining outside.

2. Vocabulary is connected with grammar, so familiarity with grammatical patterns helps the reader guess the meaning of words. For example, a word can be classified as a grammatical item or as a vocabulary item. Beautiful is a vocabulary item, and in functional grammar it is also an epithet in the nominal group the beautiful girl and reflects the speaker's opinion of the person described. The connection between vocabulary and grammar can be seen by the interdependence of grammatical and lexical cohesion. In a typical text, grammatical and lexical cohesion support each other.
3. The subject matter of a passage is interrelated and the text is often redundantly structured. To help readers, writers often give definitions or extensive clues within the text when a new word appears. So readers may have more than one chance to understand the passage.
4. By nature, reading is a process of hypothesis formation and verification; it is a communicative act between a writer and a reader (possibly a large number of readers). Consequently, the reader's understanding is unlikely to be 100 percent accurate.

   There are a number of different context clues thathelp a reader infer the meaning of a new word.

- *Morphology:* The students can derive word meanings by examining internal, morphological features, like prefixes, suffixes, and root words.
- *Reference words:* Identifying the referents of pronouns may provide a clue to the meaning of an unfamiliar word. For example, malnutrition gave him the shallowest of chests and thinnest of limbs. It stunted his growth. In this sentence, the effect of malnutrition is obvious. Students should be able to guess what malnutrition could have done to growth.

- *Cohesion:* Sometimes words in the same sentence or in adjacent sentences give an indication of the meaning of an unfamiliar word, because these words regularly co-occur with the unfamiliar word, producing what has been termed "collocational cohesion".
- *Synonyms and antonyms:* Often the reader can find the meaning of new items in the same sentence.
- *Hyponyms:* Very often the reader can see that the relationship between an unfamiliar word and a familiar word is that of a general concept accompanied by a specific example (a hyponym). For example, the museum contained almost every type of vehicle: cars, buses, trains, and even old carriages and coaches. Vehicle is being used as a hyponym; it encompasses all of the other items which are listed. Also, all of the listed items are of the same category.
- *Definitions:* Sometimes the writer defines the meaning of the word right in the text. Example: Many animals live only by killing other animals and eating them. They are called predatory animals.
- *Alternatives:* The writer may give an alternative of an unfamiliar word to make the meaning known. Example: Ichthyologists, or specialists in the study of fish, have contributed to our understanding of the past.

There are three stages of applying a context-based approach to vocabulary acquisition for adult EFL learners.

1. The teacher's first task is to draw the students' attention to cue words and phrases. Signals of connection, such as the words and and but and the phrases that is to say and in spite of, relate sentences or parts of sentences to each other. Generally, they specify "the way in which what is to follow is

systematically connected to what has gone before" .

By introducing the explicit function value of a signal word in a sentence, the teacher helps students work out the meaning of a difficult sentence or an unfamiliar word. Students become sensitive to these signals for context clues step by step, and they become skillful in identifying and using them to successfully infer meaning.

The strategies for such a pattern include recognizing the pattern and then locating the effect(s) and the cause(s). These are not always neatly arranged. Students should be told that signal words like leads to, results in, because, and caused by are used to indicate the cause-and-effect relationship.

By suggesting a few strategies to be carried out for context clues, the teacher can help students comprehend the larger chunks of information found in texts and get them over "word block."

2. The second task is to use leading questions to direct the students in a step-by-step search for context clues. With their limited experience in the target language and without the guidance of the teacher, students may find it hard to identify context cues.

   The available clues may be unnoticed or students may not be aware of words that are collocational. The teacher should use specific questions that direct the students' attention to the surrounding environment of an unknown word and that elicit responses to help focus the discussion.

   One example is to ask students to use a substitution word or expression for the unknown word. The teacher then asks if the substitution fits the context clues.

Students can revise their ideas to fit the context, probably resulting in a different substitution word. Obviously, some vocabulary development will occur when using this type of substitution strategy.

3. The third task is to prepare exercises that practice inferring the meaning of unknown words in short contexts. In the long run, it is probably more important for students to be able to explain how they infer the meaning of new words than simply to get a particular example right or wrong. In this step, the teacher selects some short paragraphs, appropriate in terms of level of difficulty, to practice strategies of inference. Each paragraph should contain one or more context clues. The teacher should ask students to infer meaning independently and then to explain how they made the inference.

The teacher provides the students with a handout of selected paragraphs of suitable length containing underlined words which are not known by the class. The students' task is to work out the meaning of the unknown words and to explain how they did it. Some students may make wrong guesses. However, they should be encouraged as long as their attempt to infer the meaning of the unknown word uses an active searching and thinking process. Sooner or later they will master the skill of developing vocabulary by inferring. There is a more advanced and elaborate type of follow-up to this kind of exercise, in which a number of unknown words are located in one passage. The learner is asked not to define the target words, but to indicate which words or phrases are helpful in inferring the meaning. There are other useful types of inference exercises that help develop the skill of inferring from context, for example, gap-filling, cloze exercises, context enrichment exercises, and word-replacement techniques.

In addition to increasing students' vocabulary, this approach has several advantages.

1. It helps readers not only learn words but also know how to use them in context. Guessing the meaning of a word from its use in context requires an understanding of semantic properties, register, and collocation. It makes readers aware of one important feature of vocabulary, namely, that context determines the meaning of words.
2. Training students to infer meaning from context gives them a powerful aid to comprehension and will speed up their reading.
3. This approach allows the learners to make intelligent, meaningful guesses. This will make the learning task much more active and challenging than direct explanation of words. It has a problem-solving characteristic that appeals to most people and challenges them to make use of their intelligence to an extent that is not always common in language classes.
4. It helps readers develop a holistic approach toward reading. Because the context of a new word may be drawn from a group of sentences, a paragraph, or even the entire text, they learn to direct their attention to language units larger than the sentence while they are looking for context clues.

## English Language in the New Age

During the 21st century, the emerging global economy reflects the availability of modern communications and production technologies in most parts of the world. So, do we need to be concerned about the future of the English language in the 21st century? According to The Economist, English continues to be the world standard language, and there is no major threat to the language or to its global popularity. But, changes are coming. Two factors drive this global marketplace. First, many manufactured products have one or more foreign components.

Ford cars and IBM computers are just two examples of this. Second, more than half of all imports and exports, which governments label foreign trade, are transacted between domestic companies and their foreign affiliates. The increasing globalization of the marketplace is forcing companies to pay more attention to international developments. Domestic firms are adjusting their structures and methods of operation to fit a broader and rapidly changing economic environment. They are increasing their geographic outreach because more of their suppliers and customers are located on various continents.

For example, last year Johnson and Johnson sold more products outside the United States than in the United States. Hewlett Packard, like many companies, lost money when the Asian economy collapsed. Joint ventures are no longer just theoretical possibilities. Mergers and acquisitions, like Chrysler/Daimler Benz and MCI and British Telecom, increasingly cross national boundaries.

This trend is expected to con-tinue into the next millennium. This internationalization is illustrated in three ways. First, companies change their basic goals to conform to a global marketplace. Second, they adapt their products to local markets. But most importantly, they do not set up international bureaucracies; instead, they hire foreign nationals who understand the local markets. English language is closely associated with this economic modernization and industrial development. Information is sent and received at increasing speed. The competitive demands of governments, industries, and corporations, both national and multinational, for technological progress require an understanding of the language of that technology—English.

The global spread of English over the last 40 years is remarkable. It is unprecedented in several ways: by the increasing number of users of the language; by its depth of penetration into societies; by its range of functions. Worldwide over 1.4 billion people live in countries where English has official status. One out of five of the world's population speaks English with some degree of competence. And by 2000 one in five—over one billion people—will also be learning English. Over 70% of the world's scientists read English. About 85% of the world's mail is written in English. And 90% of all information in the world's electronic retrieval systems is stored in English.

By 2010, the number of people who speak English as a second or foreign language will exceed the number of native speakers. This trend will certainly affect the language. English is used for more purposes than ever before. Vocabularies, grammatical forms, and ways of speaking and writing have emerged influenced by technological and scientific developments, economics and management, literature and entertainment genres. What began some 1,500 years ago as a rude language, originally spoken by obscure Germanic tribes who invaded England, now encompasses the globe. When Mexican pilots land their airplanes in France, they and the ground controllers use English. When German physicists want to alert the international scientific community to new discoveries, they first publish their findings in English. When Japanese executives conduct business with Scandinavian entrepreneurs, they negotiate in English.

When pop singers write their songs, they often use lyrics or phrases in English. When demonstrators want to alert the world to their problems, they display signs in English. Three factors continue to contribute to this spread of English: English usage in science, technology and commerce; the ability to incorporate vocabulary from other languages; and the acceptability of various English dialects. In science, English replaced German after World War II. With this technical and scientific dominance came the beginning of overall linguistic dominance, first in Europe and then globally. Today, the information age has replaced the industrial age and has compressed time and distance. This is transforming world economies from industrial production to information-based goods and services.

Ignoring geography and borders, the information revolution is redefining our world. In less than 20 years, information processing, once limited to the printed word, has given way to computers and the Internet. Computer-mediated communication is closing the gap between spoken and written English. It encourages more informal conversational language and a tolerance for diversity and individual style, and has resulted in Internet English replacing the authority of language institutes and practices. English, like many languages, uses a phonetic alphabet and fairly basic syntax. But most importantly, it has a large and extensive vocabulary, of which about 80% is foreign. Therefore, it has cognates from virtually every language in Europe and has borrowed and continues to borrow words from Spanish and French, Hebrew and Arabic, Hindi-Urdu and Bengali, Malay and Chinese, as well as languages from West Africa and Polynesia.

This language characteristic makes it unique in history. Finally, no English language central authority guards the purity of the language, therefore, many dialects have developed: American, British, Canadian, Indian, and Australian, to name a few. There is no standard pronunciation. But within this diversity is a unity of grammar and one set of core vocabulary. Thus, each country that speaks the language can inject aspects of its own culture into the usage and vocabulary. However, the future is unpredictable. As David Crystal commented, there has never been a language so widely spread or spoken by so many people as English. So, there are no precedents to help us predict what happens to a language when it achieves genuine world status.

The world is in transition, and the English language will take new forms. The language and how it is used will change, reflecting patterns of contact with other languages and the changing communication needs of people. English is divesting itself of its political and cultural connotations as more people realize that English is not the property of only a few countries. Instead, it is a vehicle that is used globally and will lead to more opportunities. It belongs to whoever uses it for whatever purpose or need. One question that arises about the future role of the English language is whether a single world standard English will develop. This could result in a supranational variety that all people would have to learn. The widespread use of English as a language of wider communication will continue to exert pressure toward global uniformity.

This could result in declining standards, language changes, and the loss of geolinguistic diversity. On the other hand, because English is the vehicle for international communication and because it forms the basis for constructing cultural identities, many local varieties could instead develop. This trend may lead to fragmentation of the language and threaten the role of English as a lingua franca. However, there have always been major differences between varieties of English. There is no reason to believe that any one other language will appear within the next 50 years to replace English.

However, it is possible that English will not keep its monopoly in the 21st century. Rather, a small number of languages may form an oligopoly—each with a special area of influence. For example, Spanish is rising because of expanding trade and the increase of the Latino population in the United States. This could create a bilingual English-Spanish region. A language shift, in which individuals change their linguistic allegiances, is another possibility. These shifts are slow and difficult to predict. But within the next 50 years, substantial language shifts could occur as economic development affects more countries.

Because of these shifts in allegiance, more languages may disappear. Those remaining will rapidly get more native speakers. This includes English. Internal migration and urbanization may restructure areas, thereby creating communities where English becomes the language of interethnic communication—a neutral language. Universities using English as the medium of instruction will expand and rapidly create a generation of middle-class professionals. Economic development will only increase the middle class, a group that is more likely to learn and use English in jobs.

# Bibliography


Bruer, J., *Schools for Thought: a science of learning in the classroom,* Cambridge, Mass.: Massachusetts Institute of Technology, 1993.

Dean, G., *Teaching Reading in Secondary Schools,* London: David Fulton Publishers Ltd., 2000.

McGilly, K., *Classroom Lessons,* Massachusetts: Massachusetts Institute of Technology, 1994.

McInerney, D. and McInerney V., *Educational Psychology-Constructing Learning,* Sydney: Prentice Hall, 1998.

Moje, E., "I Teach Students Not Subjects": Teacher-student relationships as contexts for secondary literacy, *Reading Research Quarterly* Vol 31., no. 2: 172-195, 1996.

O'Brien, D., Stewart R., and Moje E., "Why content literacy is difficult to infuse into the secondary school: complexities of curriculum, pedagogy and school culture", *Reading Research Quarterly* 30, no. 3: 442-463, 1995.

Palmer, W. P., "The Problems of Beginning School Secondary Teachers", *Papua New Guinea Journal of Education,* Vol 19, No. 2, October 1983.

______________., 'The New Teacher: Career Choice, Placement and Induction", *Papua New Guinea Journal of Education,* Vol 21, No 2, October 1985.

______________., "Higher Education, the Universities and Secondary Teacher Training in Papua New Guinea",

Education Today", *Journal of the College of Preceptors,* Vol 36, No 2, 1986.

_____________., "Beginning Secondary Teachers in PNG: Family Background, Choice of Subject and the Curriculum Needs of Schools", *paper at Fifteenth Annual South Pacific Association for Teacher Education International Conference,* Hobart, Tasmania, July 22-26, 1985

Schoenbach, R., Greenleaf C., Cziko C., and Hurwitz L., *Reading for Understanding: A Guide to Improving Reading in Middle and High School Classrooms,* San Francisco: Jossey-Bass Publishers, 1999

White, R., *Questionable Assumptions Underlying Secondary School Classrooms, SET* No.2 1993: New Zealand Council for Educational Research 1-8, 1993.

# Index